www.MeetJesus.info

Third Awakening Foundation

Book Notes

Prayer Language, Praying In the Spirit, and Tongues:
The New Testament Revelation That Changes a Believer's Life.

— Rev. Dr. Rhéma el Yérak, Sr.

Prayer Language, Praying In the Spirit, and Tongues: What Does GOD Say?

Sir Rhéma el Yérak, Sr.; DDiv.

ISBN: 978-1-7354049-7-4
Library of Congress Control Number: 2023939241
Discipleship Series: *What Does GOD Say?*: Volume 06: Advanced Level Edition

Graphic Cover Design: RC Designs
Third Awakening Foundation Inc. Publishing
ThirdAwakeningFoundation.com
Info@ThirdAwakeningFoundation.com

All Scriptures are from the *Holy Bible*: *Textus Receptus*; *Received Text*; *Standardized King James Bible 1769 A.D. (KJB)*

Cover:
"Pentecost" 1732: by Jean Restout II (1692–1768); Musée du Louvre; Paris, France.

Third Awakening Foundation

Printed in the United States of America

Dedication...

I dedicate this *Book* to my Amazing and GODly wife... the GODliest woman I have ever known. You are my Heart! There is no one else with whom I would choose to spend my life alongside. You are my anchor in this world of chaos. You have stood faithfully by my side in writing this *Book*, and many other such endeavors. You are truly my *Helpmeet*. This work would not have been possible without your support, inspiration, and dedication. I am eternally grateful. I love you more than life! Thank you for choosing me!

And to my three Sons, Granddaughter, and future generations to whom I pray to leave a legacy as a GOD-fearing man. I want to be the Father and Grandfather who chooses to stand in Truth, with humility and unshakable commitment... no matter what Evil threatens. I hope to stand shoulder-to-shoulder with each of you and together *assault* the very Gates of Hell! *ALL FOR ONE, and ONE FOR ALL!* It is truly better that we should die on our feet battling the Enemy... than to live on our knees in surrender to Evil! I pray the best for you in all that GOD has planned. To my children, as promised me by GOD, and children's children to the 7th generation. I love you with all the love a Father and Grandfather can love.

And above all, I dedicate this work to GOD who chose me before the Foundation of the World. I am but the scribe, GOD is the Author. Of this Calling I am wholly unworthy, but wholly and eternally grateful to GOD for choosing me. I am dedicated to my calling given me before the world began. In JESUS' name, Amen.

Book Notes

Table of Contents

Book Notes

Easy Reference... Helps Card...

In Order to Make This Book Easier to Read And Understand on All Levels of Christian Maturity:

1. I footnote many Bible citations and references by which the reader has the option on how far to dig-in.
2. I encourage you to read through and go back and check the footnotes.
3. Please read the Scriptures as only GOD is infallible.
4. I honor the name of JEHOVAH in lower case capitals as used in the *Received Text Bible*: JEHOVAH, JAH, LORD, GOD, etc. In the New Testament I follow the Matthew 1:21 Lowercase capitals in all references to JESUS. When quoting Scripture and other sources I keep the original formatting.
5. Occasionally I bracket a word or phrase [] when a verse or quote such as when it says "He" and insert the name that is identified before or after the reference. This saves much space in not quoting large texts to include the information that is located at a distance. You can easily go to the citation and check the reference.
6. There are instances where arrows are used to connect thoughts that are at a distance or for emphatic points. ⟷
7. My writing is to the best of my ability and as guided by the Holy Spirit I stand on 2 basic Biblical principles:
   - The *Simplicity that is in Christ Jesus*: But I fear, lest by any means, as the serpent beguiled Eve through his subtilty, so your minds should be corrupted from *the simplicity that is in Christ.* (2 Corinthians 11:3)
   - Only using doctrine that is verified in at least "two or three" witnesses in the Bible: Which things also we speak, not in the words which man's wisdom teacheth, but *which the Holy Ghost teacheth*; *comparing spiritual things with spiritual.* (1 Corinthians 2:13)
8. I have taken great lengths to simplify the text, which unfortunately, necessitates a slightly more lengthy presentation. This book is written at an 8th grade level for simplicity of understanding. However that requires a bit more time in underlining for easy focus and reference.

GOD Bless!
Rev. Dr. Rhema el Yerak

Book Notes

[1] This Helps Card is trade Marked and copyright protected by Third Awakening Foundation, Inc.

Forward...

Dear Brothers and Sisters,

I invite you on a Journey of Wonder and Amazement as we discover "*What Does GOD Say?*". This question should always be front-and-center in the Believer's heart, and before GOD, when searching the Scriptures for ... *GOD's Heart for you*!

This Discipleship Series "*What Does GOD Say?*" uses the Word of GOD to unravel and debunk the *un*godly doctrines of men, and return to the *Simplicity* in Christ JESUS. If it's not in the *Simplicity* of Christ, then it's a forgery of wicked men, and it is *not* of GOD.

Bible Study should be *Exciting* and *Awe inspiring*. Every one of these Discipleship Books in this series "*What Does GOD Say?*", I have already gone before on this same Journey. The path of this Journey leads the Believer to fulfillment in Christ, Communion with GOD, and a more Mature Christian relationship with GOD.

Keep in mind that the Level of Christian maturity that you allow GOD to grow you in this life, will determine the Level of Relationship we have with GOD in Eternity. I have determined long-ago that I will strive daily for a deeper Relationship with GOD through daily *Bible Study* and Communion with GOD. You do not want to arrive in Heaven as a stranger before the Throne! Let's Walk this higher road together and draw closer to GOD... this will impact us, and others for Eternity.

GOD Bless, and GODSpeed,

— Dr. Rhéma el Yérak

Book Notes

Introduction...

Tongues Given On Pentecost

In this *Book*, I place an emphasis on the ***Study Method*** *as revealed to me by God*, "***God's Bible Puzzle Study Method***"™[2], which God uncovered to me over decades, and thousands of hours of intensive *Bible* Study. This ***Study Method*** was gleaned directly from the *Bible*, and in close Relationship with God. For the sake of brevity, I strive to condense the name of the ***Study Method*** as often as possible.

We will see what is right, and what is wrong, and the *confusion* caused between "*praying in tongues*" and "*Praying In the Spirit*". It will surprise most Christians to learn that *only one of these is Biblical*.

In fact, only one of these 2, is an actual *Bible* Doctrine. I ask that you come to this discussion with an open mind, and a receptive heart. I pledge that we will stay wholly within *all the Constraints* of God's Holy Word. I also promise that those who take this ***Study Method*** to

[2] Often in its truncated form: **God's Perfect Bible Puzzle Study Method**™, et al. See also footnote 22.

heart, God will elevate your Christian Walk and exponentially Improve your Relationship with Him! *Read on my friend…*

Is "Tongues" Biblical? Well, …No… and Yes!
Does God have Your Attention Yet?

The *"traditions-of-men"*[3], *are traditions corrupted by sinful, and often Luciferian men, parading as real Christians*. These corruptions too often are accepted as "truth" without any questioning by Believers. Believers should *always* be *en-guard*[4] in following the Holy Spirit's *comparing-spiritual-with-spiritual*[5], by going directly to the source, God's *inerrant* Truth… His *Holy Bible*.

The *only* measurement of *Truth* (Right and Wrong) is sourced directly from God, in His Word. Using ***God's Perfect Bible Puzzle Study Method***™, the Holy Spirit will use the Word of God to *Simply* sort out all the *confusion*, and make it *Simple… Simple*[6] enough for a child to understand[7].

"Tongues" and *"Praying In the Spirit"* are two of the most *Misrepresented*, and often times *intentionally corrupted*, ***Biblical*** Doctrines targeted by *"'bible' critics"*. These ***God***-*Mockers* have *conspired* to *Deliberately Falsify and Mislead by substituting God's Word for their ungodly doctrines-of-men.*[8]

---

[3] Beware lest any man spoil you through philosophy and vain deceit, after the *tradition of men*, after the rudiments of the world, *and not after Christ*. (Colossians 2:8).
[4] A warning in combat fencing alerting your adversary that you are poised to strike.
[5] Which things also we speak, not in the words which man's wisdom teacheth, but which the Holy Ghost teacheth; *comparing spiritual things with spiritual*. (1 Corinthians 2:13).
[6] 2 Corinthians 11:3.
[7] Matthew 18:2-4; Mark 10:15.
[8] el Yerak, Dr. Rhema; Jesus and Jehovah or Yeshua and Yahweh; What Difference Does It Make What We Call God and His Son Anyway? Advanced Level Edition; chapter: The devils Who Did the Devil's Work…

"Tongues" and "Praying In the Spirit" are Two of the Most Misrepresented Doctrines of the Bible.

Many of these "'*bible*' *critics*" have ravaged the Church and continue to deceive even from beyond the grave. We can see it all around us. We may not be able to put a finger on it, but we can certainly sense something is *VERY* wrong. Virtually all of these "*critics*"[9] are not even Christians, but ravenous wolves disguised in sheep's clothing![10]

Satan is the prince of the power of the air[11] and has his tentacles *EVERYWHERE*! As the children's book *Little Red Riding Hood* warns us: The Wolf is always at the door waiting to sneak-in unawares! *Be careful for whom you open your door!*

Carefully scrutinize all *Bible* commenters and commentaries. Over 90% of "'*bible*' *critics*" and self-anointed "*theologians*" are those who "*creep in unawares*"[12] to destroy the Believers' confidence in the Word of GOD. They are in fact just evil *theorists*. Keep in mind that no *real* Christian would dare to challenge GOD on the validity of *GOD's own Word... NONE.*

Is Tongues *Biblical*? Well, No... and Yes... (I bet you didn't see that coming!) From Evangelicals, to Reformists, to Fundamentalists, to Pentecostals, to Non-Denominationalists... most Christians will be surprised at the actual *Biblical* answer to this question. This answer becomes apparent when using ***GOD's Perfect Bible Puzzle Study Method***™, so let's dive in and see and see where GOD takes us...

---

[9] See upcoming Appendix 17.1: The "Westcott & Hort Only" Controversy...

[10] Beware of false prophets, which come to you in sheep's clothing, but inwardly they are ravening wolves. (Matthew 7:15).

[11] Wherein in time past ye walked according to the course of this world, according to the prince of the power of the air, the spirit that now worketh in the children of disobedience: (Ephesians 2:2).

[12] For there are certain men crept in unawares, who were before of old ordained to this condemnation, ungodly men, turning the grace of our God into lasciviousness, and denying the only Lord God, and our Lord Jesus Christ. (Jude 1:4).

This is an *Advanced Level Discipleship Book.* Advanced Level because the subject matter can be dangerous when handled without knowing the foundational constraints, as outlined in God's Word. The *Bible* tells us that there is a lot of error in the Church. This error is dangerously promoted as "*theology*", that can destroy less learned Believers as well as unbelievers. These errors, *advanced by bad theology*, can destroy less learned Believers. Handle with care...

Bad "*theology*" is rampant in many "Christian" churches today. "*Theology*" *is from men*, and "*Doctrine*" *is from God*. The Devil is working 24/7/365 to destroy the churches from the inside out.[13] It's tragic that God can only be found in the cracks and crevasses of most modern mainline "churches". It's time to put on the Full Armor of God, and start *Fighting Back*! You *CANNOT* Win if you don't *Fight*! Contrary to children's animated movies, life is real, consequential, and the battle is not won accidently by lazy, overweight pandas!

"Theology" is from men, "Doctrine" is from God.

This is a journey to settle our spirit, and align our hearts and minds with God and His Word. In this, as in all *Biblical* endeavors, the most important question to be answered is *always*: *What Does God Say?*

Do not rely solely on preachers and teachers for your *Bible Study*. God's inerrant Wisdom trumps all of the sum total of human wisdom. As I always suggest, go directly to the Source, the *Bible*.[14] It is only by actually *reading* the Word of God, that we get Truth in Holiness and Purity. Laziness often lets us just sit in the church pew, and listen to

[13] See chapter: The devils Doing the Devil's Work...

[14] And my speech and my preaching was not with enticing words of man's wisdom, but in demonstration of the Spirit and of power: That your faith should not stand in the wisdom of men, but in the power of God. (1 Corinthians 2:4-5).

a preacher, accepting everything being spoon-fed to us[15]. Too often the spoon is laced with adulterated *false theology*. Whether we realize it or not, the *theological injury* is real and can be death by 1,000 cuts. And Yes, the Road to Hell is paved by good intensions.

We should ***always*** *Authenticate everything* we hear and read inside and outside of the *Bible*... with the *Bible*. As a major part of this ***Study*** we will delve into ***comparing-spiritual-with-spiritual***. The same is true for this *Book*, please look-up every *Bible* reference and make sure that it aligns *totally* with GOD's Word.

Because the subject of "*Tongues*" is unfamiliar to many, falsely interpreted, and demonized, the subject can be *unnecessarily confusing* to Believers. *Too many voices*, *not enough GOD*.

Too many voices, not enough GOD.

To say that allowing God the Holy Spirit to pray to God the Father, in GOD's Own Language, is somehow "not *Biblical*", is in the least sense... *dangerously unlearned*[16].

This view is of the *unlearned and used by Satan to destroy many a Believer's Walk.* As addressed specifically in this *Book*. There is an axiom that we should all keep in mind:

Don't be an Idiot, bigot, fool, nor a slave:

He, who will not reason is a bigot;
he who cannot, is a fool;
and he, who dares not, is a slave!

---

[15] I have fed you with milk, and not with meat: for hitherto ye were not able to bear it, neither yet now are ye able. (1 Corinthians 3:2).

[16] As also in all his epistles, speaking in them of these things; in which are some things hard to be understood, which they that are unlearned and unstable wrest, as they do also the other scriptures, unto their own destruction. (2 Peter 3:16).

Here are the *Commandments* of GOD:

- ✓ Come now, and let us ***reason together***, saith the LORD (Isaiah 1:18)
- ✓ My people are destroyed for ***lack of knowledge***: because thou hast rejected knowledge (Hosea 4:6)
- ✓ Though ***he wist*** [knew] ***it not***, yet is he ***guilty***, and shall bear his iniquity. (Leviticus 5:17)

Truth Only Comes From GOD

To be sure, there are several un*biblical* teachings on the subjects of "*Tongues*" and "*Praying In the Spirit*". However, that should not stop us from using the *Biblically* correct Doctrines as *verified* by GOD using ***GOD's Perfect Bible Jigsaw Puzzle Study Method***™.[17]

Specifically, don't dismiss legitimate *Bible* Doctrines out-of-hand, simply because they are unfamiliar to you. In this, we lose out on one of the greatest *Blessings* that the Believer can experience, this side of Heaven. As a matter of fact, it is a little bit of Heaven, this side of Eternity!

[17] Wow! Say that 5 times real fast!

Contrawise to the popular adage, *Un*familiarity itself often breeds contempt. Contempt in "*Tongues*" can be an arrogant way to dismiss something that is unfamiliar.[18]

The *only* argument that prevails is one Founded and Anchored in the Word of God. Men's opinions and *traditions-of-men* are *always flawed* and *corrupted* as the phrase implies. As the title of the series suggests, we must *always* go back to "*What Does God Say?*", which is only found in God's written Word, the *Bible*.

Having an emotional "*feeling*" is not equivalent to the inspiration of God. Remember Eve had a "feeling" based on an emotion in direct conflict with the expressed Word of God. Satan appealed to Eve's *rationalizing of her emotions*, not to her reasoning of the God-given facts. In reasoning the facts, God had already said *no* to Eve. Emotion was Eve looking at the fruit and saying, well it looks good to me... *Emotion is in no way a measure of Godliness*.[19]

Juxtaposing God's innate logic we can clearly deduce, as laid out here in this Book, all the aspects of *Praying in the Spirit* are *logical*. We can verify this from the Scriptures. It is a brilliant idea that no man could have "invented" on his own. We can reasonably deduce, *Prayer Language* is sourced and preordained by God.

Repetition™© [20]

A Note from the Author Here...

The chapters in this *Book* are built as *stand-alone* Study Units. Most people read a book a chapter at a time. This is a significant distinction and why each of the Books of the *Bible*, are called "*Books*". As in

[18] To dismiss these *un*familiar Doctrines, is to dismiss many similar occurrences in the Scriptures... David dancing naked, Joshua's march around Jericho, Gideon putting out a fleece, and even the Apostle Paul coming to Salvation... all were very *un*familiar circumstances with Godly inspiration and deeper implications.

[19] Colossians 2:21-23.

[20] *Subject Tracking Boxes* are ™ and © by Third Awakening Foundation Inc.

God's *Bible*, this means that in this *Book* there is a necessary, but minimal, amount of repetition and *cross-referencing between Chapters*. Primarily my highlighted and varied use of "***God's Perfect Bible Jigsaw Picture Puzzle Study Method***™"[21]. Wow that's long! Hence, I often truncate the term to a more manageable construct such as, "***God's Bible Puzzle Study Method***™"[22], and others.

There is at least one *Tracking* reminder in each chapter to help keep *continuity*, and keep from losing focus in-between Chapters. Jesus also taught using *repetition* of the most important facts. *Repetition* helps keep the crimson threads of God's Word… unbroken. *I humbly ask your indulgence on these repetitions as we begin…*

There are also a variety of emphases I use to make *Tracking* easier and *Simpler*. These include footnotes, linking arrows, bolding, color highlights for eBook subscribers, text glow, underlining, *Subject Tracking Boxes (pgs. 19-20; 37-38; 115-117, et al),* and color coding phrases like Speaking in Tongues, Tongues; Praying In the Spirit, Prayer Language, *Tongues Verification Method™,* Interpretation of Tongues; *Evil and Human Interjection*; which is all intended to make following along much easier to *Track* by the reader.

[21] Also the author's phrase, "***re***-*Version*" in its varied forms; see especially Footnote 22 following. These words are created by using poetic license, Dr. el Yerak at more accurately reflect this *Study*.

[22] Trade Marked (™) and copyrighted © ***Study Method*** by Third Awakening Foundation is referenced in several ways depending on the context. These include *Dr. el Yerak's*: ***God's Bible Puzzle Study Method***; ***Bible Jigsaw Puzzle Piece Study Method; God's Bible Jigsaw Puzzle Study Method; God's Perfect Bible Puzzle Study Method; God's Bible Jigsaw Puzzle Pieces Study Method***; ***God's Bible Picture Puzzle Study Method***; ***God's Bible Puzzle Pieces Study Method; God's Bible Jigsaw Puzzle Picture Study Method; Bible Puzzle Study Method***, *et al*.

Personal & Group Study ™©[23]

These *Discipleship Books* are written in parallel as a personal *Bible Study*, as well as a *Group Training Manual*. The *Tracking* helps are used to follow along in a Personal, or Group Discussion setting. This Book is written in multi-layered Levels to accommodate Believers at their own level, *Simple* and Easy to read. GOD tells us in His Word that everything we need to know about GOD is "*Simple*". This Book reflects this "*simplicity* that is in Christ". May you be Blessed and gain further insight into GOD and His Word. Blessings my Friend. Relax and enjoy the *Journey with JESUS*...

This *Book* is intended as a spiritual "primer". What is a "primer"? An old-fashion water pump had to be "primed" with water at the beginning to create the pressure needed to pump the water from the well. Without priming the pump, the pressure will not build to pull the water out from the well. We also need to let GOD prime our pump of ***Bible Study*** to get the Holy Water flowing.[24]

I advise that you continue ***Bible Study*** after you have finished this *Book*. These Discipleship *Books* are meant as this type of primer to allow GOD to get Believers pumped in the *flow* of the Holy Spirit using ***GOD's Bible Jigsaw Puzzle Study Method***™.

Doing the Right thing is *Simple*, but *not* always Easy.[25]

We will use the *Biblically* verified facts to reveal ***GOD's Perfect Bible Puzzle Picture***™. We will learn what the significance is between "*Praying In the Spirit*", or *Prayer Language*, from the errant "*praying in tongues*" and the "*Gift of Tongues*". The *Biblical* answers will surprise most Believers, even some who see themselves as a more mature Christian... *I know, it surprised me...*

[23] *Subject Tracking Boxes* are ™ and © by Third Awakening Foundation Inc.

[24] Water in the *Bible* is often a symbol of the Holy Spirit. Nehemiah 9:20; Isaiah 44:3; John 4:10, 7:38; *et al.*

[25] For an exhaustive study on this subject the author suggests: el Yerak, Dr Rhema; The Left's War Against GOD! and The Right's RULES FOR ANTI-RADICALS!: A Call To ACTION!: Volume 01; Master Level Edition.

Book Notes

01. The Bible's Jigsaw Puzzle… Made Simple…

God's Bible Jigsaw Puzzle Made *Simple*

We must be careful to *not* cherry-pick our theology, and stick to *only* the Doctrines found directly from the *Bible*. What we often fail to do, is understand God's Word as a *Whole*. One of my 2 basic *Biblical* foundations is always 1 Corinthians 2:13[26] which tells us that the *Holy Spirit* teaches Believers by, "*comparing spiritual things with spiritual*" wholly from the inspiration of the Holy Spirit and from the *Bible*.

God's Perfect Bible Jigsaw Puzzle Pieces Study Method™:

We will use ***God's Perfect Bible Jigsaw Puzzle Pieces Study Method™*** gleaned directly from the *Bible*, as methodized by Dr. el Yérak. We as Believers must first gather *all* the places, all the "***Puzzle Pieces***", in Scripture on any given subject. We then ensure that we have all the ***Puzzle Pieces*** that pertain to any *Biblical* subject at hand. Then "***compare***" all these *Bible* passages and make sure that all the "***Puzzle Pieces***" of ***God's Bible Puzzle Study Method™*** are on the table.

[26] And secondly, Which things also we speak, not in the words which man's wisdom teacheth, but which the Holy Ghost teacheth; comparing spiritual things with spiritual. (1 Corinthians 2:13) also But I fear, lest by any means, as the serpent beguiled Eve through his subtilty, so your minds should be corrupted from *the* ***simplicity*** *that is in Christ* (2 Corinthians 11:3).

Decently and in Order:

God always Acts Decently and In Order:

> Let all things be done *decently* and *in order*. (1 Corinthians 14:40)

God's Built-In *Bible* Dictionary:

All of God's "***Puzzle Pieces***" must then fit *Perfectly* **together**. These "***Puzzle Pieces***" cannot conflict, and once assembled, will reveal the *Whole* of ***God's Perfect Bible Puzzle Picture***™. This is ***God's Built-In Bible Dictionary***. Through this ***Study Method***, Believers can minimize any errant "*theological*" or personal biases *infecting their theology*. The *Bible* is God's, and not man's to interpret with one's personal bias, nor is it of any private interpretation.[27]

If we have properly arranged all of "***God's Puzzle Pieces***" of Scripture, and assembled ***God's Bible* Jigsaw *Puzzle Picture***™, and we still either have pieces left over, or holes with no "*Piece*" to fill it, *we are missing something, not God.*

When starting a new jigsaw puzzle, virtually all people correctly begin with the outermost boundaries at the edge first. The outer pieces are distinguished by a straight edge. Likewise, the ***God's Bible Puzzle Study Method***™ collects all of ***God's Puzzle Pieces***, and begins with the outer edges, which establishes the outer Boundaries. Like a tabletop jigsaw puzzle, nothing can *Fall*[28] outside of the boundaries,

[27] Knowing this first, that no prophecy of the scripture is of any private interpretation. (2 Peter 1:20).

[28] This is an intentional reference to mankind "Falling" from Grace when Adam and Eve rebelled against God and were kicked out of the Garden of Eden. Always make sure that your *Bible* Study never Falls outside of God's preset parameters.

which is ensured by properly using ***GOD's Bible Puzzle Study Method***™. This is a time-proven ***Study Method***. When properly employed, it will always yield ***GOD's Perfect Puzzle Picture***™!

There can be no truncating of verses, no trimming *Puzzle Pieces*, to make something "fit" in **GOD's *Perfect Bible Jigsaw Puzzle Study Method***™. When applying GOD's "*comparing spiritual things with spiritual*", with proper *Bible* Studying, all of the imagined *Bible* "contradictions" and "confusion", *abruptly disappear*!

Too Many Theologians, Not Enough GOD

This truncating or "abridging" of Scripture is also commonly referred to as "cherry-picking". Cherry-picking is as JESUS warns us of, the foundation built upon the sand[29], at any challenge, the house will Fall down! On the sand, is where all "'*bible' cults*"[30] and many Heathen religions are built. GOD's Perfect Word is a *Perfect Whole*.

Sadly, some *invent* a hypothesis, and then seek to reverse-engineer it with their own *predetermined biases*. It is any wonder then, that so many Believers are *confused*?

All the ***Pieces*** of ***GOD's Bible Puzzle Pieces Study Method***™ makes all the "***Pieces***", or *Bible* passages, fit *flawlessly* together and yield ***GOD's Wholly Complete Perfect Puzzle Picture***™. Too often *Puzzle Pieces* are forced when assembling the *Bible*, people (*Bible*-scoffing "scholars",

[29] Matthew 7:26-27.

[30] Scientology, Jehovah's Witnesses, Mormons, *et al.*

worldly "intellectuals", atheistic mythologists, and *Bible* manipulators) *predetermine* ***what*** they think *God should have said*, and *Who God should be*. In direct opposition, ***God has a place for everything, and everything in its place.***[31]

When you start from an assumption, and try to get God to join in on your *traditions-of-men*, the results are alien from God. We should let God work through us, as *nothing works unless God is working through the Believer*. God tells us what He wants, and when we follow God's errorless Word, Godly results are guaranteed.

Sometimes We Forget That It's All About God.
We're Just The Conduit Through Which God
Accomplishes His Will.

Sometimes we forget that, *"it's all about God"*. Believers are just there as a *conduit* through which God accomplishes His will. Always seek God's will so we don't embarrass ourselves, embarrass God, or harm them to whom we are ministering. *We are being watched*[32]...

This getting ahead of God could potentially discourage the one being prayed over. If we, without direction from God, pray for someone to be healed, and when they are not healed, we make God look powerless. We embarrass ourselves and God. This is a form of self-righteousness, whether we realize it or not:

> For they being ignorant of God's righteousness, and going about to establish their *own righteousness*, *have not submitted themselves unto the righteousness of God*. (Romans 10:3)

[31] In the case of the aforementioned violators, their proper place is Hell.

[32] Wherefore seeing we also are compassed about with so great a cloud of witnesses, let us lay aside every weight, and the sin which doth so easily beset us, and let us run with patience the race that is set before us, (Hebrews 12:1).

This results in discouragement and a sense of not being worthy before GOD. It makes people question if GOD really does love them. This is what happens when we try to get out ahead of GOD![33]

Just as a tabletop jigsaw puzzle has a picture on the box cover that predetermines the final assembled picture, we have to put all of ***GOD's Bible Puzzle Pieces***™ together to see ***GOD's Whole Perfect Puzzle Picture***™. GOD's Word has a Predetermined *Picture which* reflects the Word of GOD as a *Whole*, not in incomplete and disjointed *pieces*.

As we progress through ***GOD's Bible Jigsaw Puzzle Pieces Study Method***™ we see GOD more and more clearly. This in putting all of **GOD's Puzzle *Pieces***™ in their proper place. Relying on just individual Pieces renders an incomplete, truncated, and deceptive picture.

Tear It Apart…

A final ***GODly Puzzle Picture***™ will reveal a complete, ***Perfect***, and ***GODly Picture***™. An unGodly puzzle picture will give you a distorted and corrupted *inverse* picture. Remember if there are Holes of

Holes In your Puzzle Are Holes In Your Armor!

Assumption in using ***GOD's Bible Puzzle Study Method***™, or *Pieces* left over, your picture is *not* the GODly picture. *You then must tear apart*

[33] A good measure of when to act is asking GOD for "Wisdom and Opportunity". Wisdom to know how to act, and Opportunity to know when to act. This formula keeps the biases at bey and out of the equation leaving GOD to do what He wants, and when He wants it.

your corrupted puzzle and start all over again! Too often our human biases cause us to end up with a *corrupt* puzzle picture. People ignore their corruption at their own peril, and the vicarious destruction of others.

Problems Assembling ***God's* Bible Puzzle**™ are fully our mistake, and *never* God's mistake:
Sometimes we just have to tear apart our errant puzzle... and start all over again. *Starting again is the price we must pay in cutting through the "theology" fog to reveal God's unobscured Truth.* The Truth is Easy to see once **God's *Bible Jigsaw Puzzle Study Method***™ is properly used to complete ***God's Perfect Puzzle Picture***™.

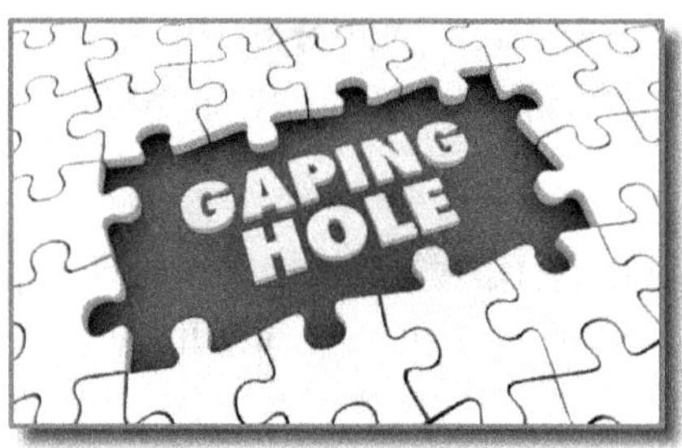

No Holes

One of the Most Egregious Sins *Against* God[34] is... *Betrayal.*
By *betrayal* I mean, among other things, *denominations* using their handed down "*theology*" or "*traditions-of-men*", which is a *betrayal* Against God[35], and His Holy Word. This is as Evil as Judas Iscariot's betrayal of Jesus. Remember, Jesus is the Word of God[36].

These denominational manuals are "*men's theology*", which almost *never* actually represents God's **Perfect** Doctrine. In putting ***God's Perfect Bible Puzzle Picture***™ together, we should unerringly avoid

[34] See also the author's Book: el Yerak, Dr Rhema; The Left's War Against God! and The Right's RULES FOR ANTI-RADICALS!: A Call To ACTION! Volume 01; Master Level Edition.
[35] For Betrayal see the author's Book: el Yerak, Dr Rhema; *Communion: What Does God Say?.*
[36] John 1:1-17.

these "*traditions-of-men*", which is *men's corrupted* and *invented* "*theology*". Let the Holy Spirit teach you GOD's Doctrine and alert you to any corrupt theology of men that you may have already internalized.

Through 8-years of cloistered monastic *Bible* Study, I have had the rare opportunity to delve deeply and directly into GOD's Word... 12-hours a day, 7-days a week. I was raised in a Christian Church and was stunned at the sheer volume of false theology in which I had been indoctrinated. Christianity had always seemed a bit stiff and hollow to me. I was definitely Born-Again, but the *Power* of GOD had always seemed just out of reach.

I have had to replace my "*theology*" with proper *Bible* "*Doctrine*", many, many times. As the saying goes, The more you know, the more you know you don't know. As my ***Bible* Study** continues, I have to humbly and continually replace my man-made "*theology*", with the "*Doctrines* of GOD", from His infallible Word.

It is telling that the *Webster's Thesaurus* equates the word "*puzzle*" with "*problem*". You are literally "*problem solving*" *spiritual* "*problems*" in properly using ***GOD's Bible Puzzle Study Method***™.

Webster's Thesaurus equates "puzzle" *with* "problem". *We solve spiritual problems.*

A Further Note of Caution...

Please do not solely rely on *Bible* "scholars", theologians, celebrity preachers, many evangelical preachers, and the like, for your *Bible* Study and conclusions. Their "puzzle pieces", more often than not, reflect an Evil, mirror opposite puzzle of rebellion standing wholly *Against*[37]....... ***GOD's Perfect Puzzle Masterpiece***™.

[37] El Yerak, Dr. Rhema; The Left's War Against GOD! and The Right's RULES FOR ANTI-RADICALS!: A Call To ACTION!; Volume 01; Master Level Edition.

These atheistic mythologists, *Bible*-Manipulators, *Bible*-scoffers are a bed of vipers working to seal the destruction of God's people. Rely only on God and His Word and ***God's Perfect Puzzle Study Method***™. This is why I build exclusively on God's Word, necessarily involving dozens and sometimes hundreds of embedded Scriptures.

Satan Inversely mocks God's Perfect Puzzle™
making sin look "godly" in reflecting Satan's
mirror opposite puzzle of rebellion.

Satan *Inversely Imitates and Mocks* Everything of God:

Satanists have a *Black Sabbath*, an *Evil Communion*, and an *Evil puzzle maker*. Evil *inverts* and mocks ***God's Perfect Puzzle Study Method***™:

> For they *eat the bread* of *wickedness*, and *drink the wine* of *violence*. (Proverbs 4:17)

This is What the Apostle Paul Says About Learning the Truth of Scripture from Other Men:

> To reveal his Son [Jesus] in me, that I might preach him among the heathen; *immediately I conferred not with flesh and blood*: *Neither* went I up to Jerusalem *to them which were apostles before me*; but *I went into Arabia* [to Jesus in the wilderness], and returned again unto Damascus. (Galatians 1:16-17)

The Apostle Paul communed and learned directly, and exclusively from Jesus in the wilderness[38].

Paul received this New Revelation of the New Testament from God Himself. *Wow*! The *Bible* Canon is now closed and there are no

---

[38] Galilaeans 1:12.

further additions to God's Word[39]. We should follow Paul's example[40] and get our Doctrine directly from the Source, which is exclusively God's Word.

A significant part of a Believer chasing after God is getting into the details of His Word. *Bible* Study is *Simple, but not always Easy*, nor quick.

I've always told my children. You've gotta want it! You have to pay the price[41] of letting God purge your sin and grow your Faith[42]. It's the same with our relationship with God... *You've gotta want it!* It's always a painful process. The more you want it, the more God is able purge and refill.

Life with God is an Adventure...
Enjoy the Journey...

[39] Revelation 22:18.
[40] 2 Thessalonians 3:9.
[41] See author's upcoming Books: Paying the Price: What Does God Say?; and Grow UP!: What Does God Say?.
[42] el Yerak, Dr Rhema; WALKING BY FAITH... What Is Faith, How To Live By Faith, and Finally Living the Victorious Christian Life!; Discipleship Series: Volume 02: Advanced Level.

Book Notes

02. Confusion In the Church...

Confusion In the Church?

We will explore what the *Bible* says about the *misrepresentation* and imaginary "*praying in tongues*". You will likely be surprised by what the *Bible actually* has to say! However, *you will also be Blessed and Set Free by the time you finish this Book....*

---

praying in tongues is one of the most controversial doctrines in the Church today. It's controversial for a good reason: There Is No Such Thing!

Has God gotten your attention yet?
Read on and I guarantee you will be Blessed and glad you did...

These are 2 Separate and Distinct Biblical Doctrines:
It is absolutely necessary that we understand that these are 2 separate manifestations of the Holy Spirit, "*Tongues*" and "*Prayer Language*". These are maliciously and venomously lumped together

as "*praying in tongues*". This makes it appear that these 2 separate Doctrines are the same Doctrine, which in turn creates great *confusion* in the pews. *Only Satan is the author of confusion.* This misinterpretation creates a rupture in the Church, because it is *not* of God, and it is an *abominational theology* straight from the *Pit of Hell*!

Believers Speak to People and Pray to God.

"*Speaking In Tongues*" and "*Praying In the Spirit*" are not the same Doctrine of God, often wrongfully swapped for "*praying in tongues*".

The Two ***Actual*** ***Biblical*** Manifestations of the Holy Spirit are:

1. *Speaking* in Tongues/*Tongues*
2. *Praying* In the Spirit/*Prayer Language*.

Because of the great *confusion* caused by the widespread *misinterpretation* of the Scriptures, we will refer to #1 as "***Speaking*** in Tongues" or just "Tongues"[43]; And #2 as either "***Praying*** In the Spirit", or "***Prayer*** *Language*".[44]

These terms will help us keep these 2 Doctrines, as God does, *separate* and *mutually exclusive*. We must be very careful to keep our interpretation using the entire context of the passages using ***God's Jigsaw Puzzle Picture Study Method***™, which is designed to

[43] ("*Speaking In Tongues*" is the *verb* form; and "*Tongues*" is the *noun* form.)

[44] ("*Praying* In the Spirit" is the *verb* form, and "*Prayer Language*" is the *noun* form.)

methodically keep our eyes on the *Bible* as a Whole, and *off of men's biases and corruption*. *Confusion* is *caused by the non-existent* "*praying in tongues*" in Church, which *unavoidably* results in *confusion*. Judging by this *confusion*, we can *know* that it's *not* of GOD:

> For *God is not the author of confusion*, but of peace, as in all churches of the saints. (1 Corinthians 14:33).

Confusion from Competing Voices

Have you ever been in a Church setting where someone stood up and blurted out strange sounds pretending to be "*praying in tongues*"? Were you *uncomfortable* in your spirit? Did it leave you feeling *confused* and a bit *repulsed*?

This type of confusion is endemic of a demonic spirit, and *not* of GOD's Holy Spirit. Demons *imitate* and *mock* GOD's ways to sow *Confusion* and *Destruction* in the Church:

> Beloved, *believe not every spirit*, ***but*** *try the spirits whether they are of God*: because many false prophets are gone out into the world. (1 John 4:1).

Satan's False Equivalent

The image above is a prime example of how Satan *transposes* the Luciferian Egyptian "sun god" (Satan), in place of God the Holy Spirit. Did you catch that *subtilty* of Satan's *substitution* of Evil for GOOD? Remember the Holy Spirit is our Comforter,[45] *not our trickster*.

Satan is very Clever...
Satan substitutes the True Doctrines of GOD, for the Luciferian "*traditions-of-men*".

> But I fear, lest by any means, *as the serpent **beguiled** Eve through his **subtilty**, so your minds should be **corrupted** from the simplicity that is in Christ*. (2 Corinthians 11:3)

The Holy Spirit Is the Believer's Comforter

If Believers seem *confused* and *uneasy*, take pause and weigh it in the Holy Spirit indwelling your spirit, and also always in GOD's Word first. By the time you finish this *Book*, you will be equipped to overcome *false theology* and learn to experience the *Peace* of the Holy Spirit. We will flesh out "*Tongues*" and "*Praying In the Spirit*", *as* the *trickery* it actually is, of the ungodly "*praying in tongues*".

We will deeply explore the *Biblical* fact that what is commonly, and *falsely*, referred to as "*praying in tongues*", does not exist in GOD's Holy Word. Again, the *misrepresentation* of "*praying in tongues*" is a false *doctrine-of-men*. Believers cannot "*pray in tongues*", as it *does not exist* in the *Bible*. But, all Believers can "*Pray in the Spirit*".

[45] John 14:16-17, 26.

Important:

We will show a clear separation of the 2 actual *Bible* Doctrines. "Tongues" is a *Gift* of the Holy Spirit given only to a *few* Christians, whereas "*Prayer Language*" is for *all* Christians. Furthermore, we will see that "*Praying In the Spirit*" is *Commanded*[46] by GOD for *all* Christians to use 24/7/365. *Yep, you read that correctly, read on...*

Prayer Language & Tongues Made *Simple*™©[47]

Are You Confused?
Yeah, that's Satan's intention.........

Simplified:

"*Speaking* in Tongues" is a Believer *Speaking to Unbelievers*

"*Praying* In the Spirit" is the Believer *Praying to GOD*.

> Wherefore *tongues* are for a sign, not to them that believe, but *to them that believe not*: but *prophesying* serveth not for them that believe not, but for them which believe. (1 Corinthians 14:22)[48]

It might seem messy, but GOD helps us identify the false blur and bring order out of our chaos. *It's the Journey≈≈≈≈ that brings us closer to GOD.* GOD gives us all of His ***Puzzle Pieces***™, for those who seek GOD... they will find GOD assembling ***GOD's Puzzle Pieces***™ to Reveal GOD's ***Perfect Picture***™ of His Excellency in the ***Perfect Bible Puzzle Picture***™.

We must be diligent in *differentiating* between GOD's Doctrines of "*Speaking* In Tongues" and "*Praying* In the Spirit". Using ***GOD's Jigsaw Puzzle Picture Method***™ we discover that there are a few *Biblical* instances where the phrase "*Speaking* In Tongues" must be interpreted using ***GOD's Bible Jigsaw Puzzle Study Method***™, as "*Praying* In the Spirit".

[46] For "Commanded" see chapter: Believers Commanded to Use Prayer Language!

[47] *Subject Tracking Boxes* are ™ and © by Third Awakening Foundation Inc.

[48] This verse is quoted 2 more times for 3 different emphases.

For Instance...

> For he that speaketh *in an unknown tongue speaketh not unto men, but unto God*: for no *man understandeth him*; howbeit *in the spirit he speaketh mysteries*. (1 Corinthians 14:2)

Believers "Speak" to people and *"Pray" to God*. 1 Corinthians 14:2 is *"Prayer Language"*, not *"Tongues"*. Many of the cherry-picking heresies that we have discussed, involve clipping small *Bible* phrases and making it a deceptive *commandment-of-men*. To find these nuances we must diligently apply ***God's Bible Jigsaw Puzzle Study Method***™ to flesh out every ***Bible Puzzle Piece***™, while *wholly comparing-spiritual-with-spiritual*.

A *fail-safe* way to avoid this *confusion* is to use ***God's Bible Puzzle Study Method***™. When you put all the *Bible Puzzle Pieces* on the table and *wholly compare-spiritual-with-spiritual*[49], you get the whole ***Precise Picture***™ of God's intended ***Picture***. Follow ***God's*** instructions and you get ***God's Perfect Puzzle Box Cover Picture*** ™.

Clarifying and separating "*Speaking* In Tongues" and "*Praying* In the Spirit" brings Peace, Freedom, *Boldness*, and *Power* to the Believer.

Peace is one *Biblical* measure of the validity of a Christian practice. The primary source of the measure of what is right, and what is wrong, is the whole and total content of the *Biblical* text. Following the actual instructions using ***God's Bible Puzzle Pieces Study Method***™ the actual instructions using ***God's Bible Puzzle Pieces Study Method***™ brings God's *Peace*, and not Satan's *confusion*.

[49] Which things also we speak, not in the words which man's wisdom teacheth, but which the Holy Ghost teacheth; comparing spiritual things with spiritual. (1 Corinthians 2:13).

03. *Gifts of Tongues & Interpretation of Tongues*

A *Gift* of the Holy Spirit

As we begin our discussion, we need to recognize that there is.......... *No such thing* as "*praying in tongues*". (...point made?) This point will become abundantly clear in the next three chapters by using the time-tested, *Bible* based, ***God's Bible Puzzle Pieces Study Method***™.[50] Because of a maelstrom of *misinterpretation* and *misdirection*, *confusion* abounds in the Church and has metastasized into fractures between Believers and congregations. Let's see, "*What Does God Say?*".

These 2 Doctrines in question are "Speaking in Tongues" and "Praying In the Spirit".[51] We will unravel the bad theology of "*praying in tongues*" using only God's Holy Word.

As previously noted, "*praying in tongues*" is *not* a sign of Salvation[52], *nor* a *Biblical* Gift of the Holy Spirit. However, "*Praying In the Spirit*" is a sign of *being baptized for ministry by the Holy Spirit*. To be Baptized by the Holy Spirit for ministry can *only* happen to a Born-Again Believer.

[50] See the chapter The Bible's Jigsaw Puzzle... Made Simple.

[51] See a wider discussion in chapter: Prayer Language and Spiritual Warfare.

[52] For a broader discussion see chapter: Tongues Not a Required to Confirm Salvation.

How to Receive the *Empowerment* of the Holy Spirit:
The Believer is responsible to hold up his, or her, part of Faith[53] in the manifestation of the Gifts of the Holy Spirit:

> Wherefore I put thee in remembrance that *thou stir up* [*rekindle*] *the gift of God*, which is in thee by the putting on of my hands. (2 Timothy 1:6)

Jesus Prophesied the Upcoming New Testament *Speaking in Tongues*:

> And these signs *will* [in the future[54]] *accompany those who have believed*: in My name; they will cast out demons, they will *speak* with new *tongues*. (Mark 16:17).

Those refuting the validity of "*Speaking in Tongues*" are simply standing against the Words of Jesus and the Holy Scriptures. The *Bible* repeatedly shows the difference between "*Speaking In Tongues*" and "*Praying In the Spirit*".[55] As good stewards of God's Word, we *must* learn to properly apply the Gifts of the Holy Spirit:

> Nevertheless I tell you the truth; It is expedient for you that I go away: for if I go not away, the Comforter [Holy Spirit[56]] will not come unto you; but if I depart, I will send him unto you. (John 16:7)

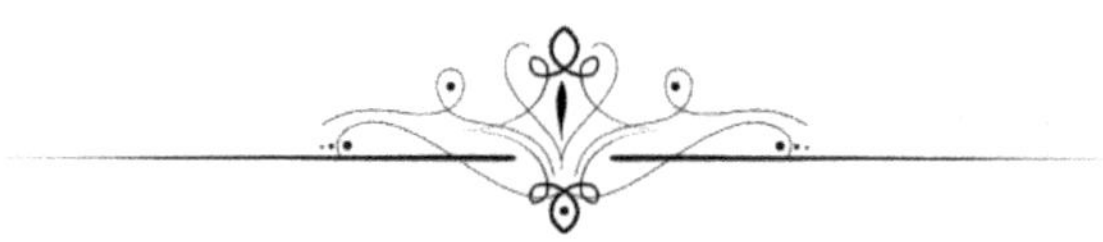

[53] el Yerak, Dr Rhema; WALKING BY FAITH... What Is Faith, How To Live By Faith, and Finally Living the Victorious Christian Life!; Discipleship Series: Volume 02: Advanced Level.
[54] See Acts 2:1 and following.
[55] See upcoming Chapters: Ephesians Chapter 6: Spiritual Warfare; and *1 Corinthians Chapter 14: Made Simple*.
[56] But the Comforter, which is the Holy Ghost, whom the Father will send in my name, he shall teach you all things, and bring all things to your remembrance, whatsoever I have said unto you. (John 14:26).

The Day of Pentecost

The "Gift" of the Manifestation of Speaking in Tongues Began…

… the First Day of the New Testament, the First Pentecost, when the Holy Spirit fell on certain Christians who began *Speaking with Tongues*, as willed by the Holy Spirit:

> While Peter yet spake these words, *the Holy Ghost fell on all them* which heard the word. And they of the circumcision which believed were astonished, as many as came with Peter, because that on the Gentiles also was poured out **the** *gift of the Holy Ghost*. For they heard them *speak with tongues* [existing foreign languages], and magnify God. (Acts 10:44-46).

Notice as you read, this is "*Speaking in Tongues*", not "~~*praying in tongues*~~". It should also be noted that those Christians who were given the Gift of "*Speaking in Tongues*", are not again noted to have exercised this Gift. It seems that the Gift of "*Speaking In Tongues*" may be a *temporary* Gift for specific Believers, given for a specific time, for witnessing Salvation, throughout the Church Age.

Tongues and *Prayer Language* Made *Simple*:

- 1 Corinthians 12 describes gifts including: "*Tongues*" and "*Interpretation of Tongues*"
- 1 Corinthians 13 is on "*Charity*", God's *Agape* Love.
- 1 Corinthians 14 is the differentiation of "*Praying In the Spirit*" and "*Tongues*" so that there would be *no confusion* between them.

Here is the Foundation in Scripture that Helps Us *Differentiate* between "*Speaking* In Tongues" and "*Praying In the Spirit*":
The Gift of "*Speaking In Tongues*" *is ONLY for witnessing Salvation of Jesus Christ in a natural tongue*, or natural earthly *language*, *which the hearer understands*. The First Day of the New Testament times:

> And there appeared unto them cloven tongues like as of fire, and it sat upon each of them. And they were all filled with the Holy Spirit and began *to speak in other tongues*, as the Spirit gave [**Gifted**] them **utterance**. And there were dwelling at Jerusalem Jews, devout men, out of every nation under heaven. Now when this was noised abroad, the multitude came together, and were confounded, *because that every man heard them speak **in his own language***. And they were all amazed and marvelled, saying one to another, Behold, are not all these which speak Galilaeans? And *how hear we every man in our **own tongue*** [human language], wherein we were born? Parthians, and Medes, and Elamites, and the dwellers in Mesopotamia, and in Judaea, and Cappadocia, in Pontus, and Asia, Phrygia, and Pamphylia, in Egypt, and in the parts of Libya about Cyrene, and strangers of Rome, Jews and proselytes, Cretes and Arabians, *we do hear them **speak in our tongues*** [native languages] *the wonderful works of God*. (Acts 2:3-11).

The "*Gift of Tongues*" is *Only* made Possible by the Indwelling of the Holy Spirit:

> And they were all filled with the *Holy Ghost*, and (then⇨⇨⇨) began to *speak with other tongues*, as the *[Holy]* ***Spirit*** *gave them **utterance***. (Acts 2:4)

> To another the working of miracles; to another prophecy; to another discerning of spirits; to another *divers kinds of tongues*; to another the *interpretation of tongues* (1 Corinthians 12:10)

What is Commonly Referred to simply as "**Tongues**" (*noun form*) of the, "***Gift***" of the **Holy Spirit** to only a *few* Select Believers:

> While Peter yet spake these words, the Holy Ghost fell on all them which heard the word. And they of the circumcision which believed were astonished, as many as came with Peter, because that on the Gentiles also was poured out *the **gift** of the **Holy Ghost***. For they heard them ***speak with tongues***, and magnify God. Then answered Peter, Can any man forbid water, that these should not be baptized, which have received the Holy Ghost as well as we? (Acts 10:44-47)

The *Gift* of Tongues:

The *Gift of Tongues* is a "*Gift*" from the Holy *Spirit*. This "*Gift*" is an *extra-ordinary Gift* given *only to some*[57] Believers, for certain times. This "Gift of Tongues" (*noun form*), also called "***Speaking In Tongues***", (*verb form*) is only given for extraordinary (*extra-ordinary*) circumstances for witnessing of JESUS' Salvation to the unsaved in their own native language:

> And there are *diversities* [*differences*] of operations, but it is the same God which worketh all in all. But the *manifestation of the Spirit* is given to every man to profit withal [***all** the Body*]. For *to one* is *given by the Spirit* the word of wisdom; to another the word of knowledge by the same Spirit; To another faith by the same Spirit; to another the gifts of healing by the same Spirit; To another the working of miracles; to another prophecy; to another discerning of spirits; to *another divers* [*different*] kinds of **tongues**; *to another the **interpretation of tongues***: But all these worketh that one and the selfsame Spirit, *dividing to every man severally as he will*. For as the body is one, and hath many members, and all the members of that one body, being many, are one body: so also is Christ. (1 Corinthians 12:6-12)

[57] 1 Corinthians 12:7.

The *Gift* of the "*Interpretation of Tongues*":
The *Gift* of "*Tongues*", (*noun*) which is the *Gift* of "*Speaking In Tongues*" (*verb*), is using a preexisting foreign human language used *only* to witness Salvation in Christ JESUS to the unsaved, and to glorify GOD as another form of Witnessing to non-believers who do not understand your native "tongue".

The *Gift* of the "*Interpretation of Tongues*" is GOD's *safeguard* against someone claiming to be "Speaking in Tongues", but may actually be blaspheming GOD. How else would we know that it was an actual *Gift* being used, unless of course, it could be ***verified by a different** Believer through the Holy Spirit's Gift* of the "*Interpretation of Tongues*"?

An "*Interrupter*" is GOD's *failsafe* mechanism to identify a deceptive "*speaking in tongues*". If you have ever been in a church and felt terribly uncomfortable at someone using "*tongues*", then it is most likely, that the indwelling *Holy Spirit is sending up warning flares in your spirit*.

An "*Interpreter of Tongues*" is *only* for Interrupting a foreign Tongue, a human foreign language. It is used to *verify* the legitimacy of the Believer claiming to be "Speaking in Tongues", or its more obvious imposter of "*praying-in-tongues*". If there is no "*Interrupter of the Tongues*", *then the speaker is NOT "Speaking in Tongues*". GOD connects these *2 different Gifts* and foresees when to make it work.

This *failsafe*, when used correctly, will *expose* every person claiming that they are "*praying in tongues*" when they are *not*! When in fact, they are just muttering gibberish, or worse, blaspheming GOD with no Church *Safeguards*. There have always been many false "Believers" in the Church. The Apostle Paul warned us:

> For I know this, that after my departing *shall grievous wolves enter in among you*, *not sparing the flock*. (Acts 20:29)

A 2 to 3 Member Ministry "Team" for Legitimate "*Interpretation*":
Keep in mind that the *Gift* of the "*Interpretation of Tongues*" is:

1). *A Believer Interpreting an existing human language* (i.e. English, Hebrew, Mandarin, Spanish, *et al.*[58]) of someone claiming to be "*Speaking In Tongues*". The "*Interpretation of Tongues*" *is always and only used alongside a Believer "Speaking In Tongues"*. For the single purpose of witnessing Salvation in Christ JESUS in the unbeliever's understandable language. (and to glorify GOD in Witnessing JESUS)

2). There can be only be *one "Interpreter of Tongues"* who speaks GOD's *Interpretation out-loud*. (Otherwise you would need another "*interrupter*" to "*Interrupt*" the first "*Interpreter*"... Ring around, ring around Rose...)

There is a *Two Person Believer Minimum for Tongues and Verification of Tongues*, including: the *Speaker of Tongues*, the *Interpreter of Tongues*, and if possible, a *silent* 3rd Observer in *training* to become either a "*Speaker*", and/or an "*Interpreter*", or last minute stand-in. The *4th person* is the *un*saved being witnessed to by 2 or 3 Believers.

The 3rd Person, a Believer, in "Standby" Mode:
The 3rd person is *not just standing-by*, but also *training on the side while observing in silence*. This is the 3rd Believer mentioned in the following verse.

To give some closure to the previous chapter, "*Confusion In the Church*", there is a *minimum of 2* and *maximum of 3 Believers, and the 4th being the "unbeliever" to whom you are witnessing, a maximum of 4 people*.

[58] Now when this was noised abroad, the multitude came together, and were confounded, because that every man heard them speak in his own language. And how hear we every man in our own tongue, wherein we were born? Parthians, and Medes, and Elamites, and the dwellers in Mesopotamia, and in Judaea, and Cappadocia, in Pontus, and Asia, Phrygia, and Pamphylia, in Egypt, and in the parts of Libya about Cyrene, and strangers of Rome, Jews and proselytes, Cretes and Arabians, *we do hear them speak in our tongues* the wonderful works of God. (Acts 2:6-11).

> If any man speak in an unknown tongue, let it be *by two*, or at the most *by three*, and that by course; and let *one interpret*. (1 Corinthians 14:27)

If there would be more than 1 active *Interpreter*, then one of the "*Interpreters*" could introduce *confusion* if the 2nd "*Interpreter of Tongues*" *conflicted* with the primary *Interpreter of Tongues*. (Now that's confusing!) God hates confusion as it's not of God. *But wait…*

⚠ Use Extreme *Caution* when Choosing an *Interpreter*:
This choice will be a *direct Reflection on God*. Care should be employed vetting a potential "*Interpreter of Tongues*". There are many, many wolves among the sheep whose assignment is to sow *confusion*, doubt, and discord into the Christian body.[59] One telltale sign of an unqualified "interpreter" is if they go by "*feeling*" not by the "Book", the Book is the *Bible*.

No Interrupter, No Tongues…

No Interpreter, No Tongues:
God clearly differentiates "*Speaking in Tongues*" from "*Praying In the Spirit*". Without a legitimate "*Interpreter*", *keep silent* do not even attempt to Speak In Tongues:

> But if there be *no Interpreter*, *let him keep silence* in the church; and let him *speak* [*only*[*to himself*, and **to God** [*Prayer Language*]. (1 Corinthians 14:28)

The Devil strives to create *division* among the Brethren. *Interpretation* ***needs to be handled with extreme Care***. In ministering in Jesus' stead, we cannot consider the "feelings" and reaction of the

---

[59] Now I beseech you, brethren, mark them which cause ***divisions*** and ***offences*** contrary to the doctrine which ye have learned; and ***avoid them***. (Romans 16:17).

"*Interpreter*" if it becomes necessary to dismiss an *Interpreter* and replace this *Interpreter* with the 3rd Believer keep ***SILENT*** while in *standby*, and in the on-the-job training.

This can be done tactfully, however, this type of Intersession, when possible, needs to be handled ahead of time to eliminate the evil environment *before you begin*. And *you might need the 3rd Believer in standby on the side to step in if necessary*. Always keep in mind that you as the "*Speaker of Tongues*" represents God, standing literally in Jesus' place.[60]

Keep in Mind that this is All About:

(Follow the red brick road: ⇨)

⇨ 1). the ***Unbeliever*** that needs to hear about Salvation

⇨ 2). ***The** 1st*, a Believer "*Speaker of Tongues*"

⇨ 3). ***The** 2nd*, a Believer "*Interpreter of Tongues*"

⇨ 4). ***The** 3rd*, a Believer a ***standby Believer training*** and/or to step-in as a backup "*Interpreter of Tongues*".

God is a Triune God. The Three in One Godhead. *With less than two Believers there is no Godly verification.* Everything is meaningless without the *Interpreter of Tongues*.

Again, No Interpreter, No Tongues.

God knows the human predisposition of seeking people's own vain glory, where a person will blow-by God's established perimeters if left unrestrained.

Less than two Believers, there is no Holy Spirit in the middle... Interpreting the word into the *Interpreter's* spirit. To perform the

[60] Now then we are ambassadors for Christ, as though God did beseech you by us: we pray you in Christ's stead, be ye reconciled to God. (2 Corinthians 5:20).

miracle of the "*Gift of Interpretation*":

> How shall we escape, *if we neglect so great [#2] salvation*; which at the first began to be [**#1**] *spoken* [*Rhema* Words] *by the Lord*, and was [**#3**] ***confirmed*** *unto us by them that heard him*; God also bearing them witness, both with signs and wonders, and with divers miracles, and *gifts of the* ***Holy Ghost***, according to his own will? (Hebrews 2:3-4)

The Gifts of the "*Interpretation of Tongues*" and "Speaking In Tongues" are *Never* Given to The Same Believer... *NEVER!*:
In case you missed it the Gifts of "*Interpretation of Tongues*" and "*Speaking In Tongues*" are *NEVER given to the same Believer*. If both Gifts were given together to the same Believer, then there is *NO outside confirmation of the Interpretation*, and *no verification* of *legitimacy* of the "*Speaking in Tongues*". The repeated use of the word "***another***" demonstrates these 2 are different "***one-****from-****another***".

> To another the working of miracles; to ***another*** prophecy; to another discerning of spirits; to ***another*** *divers kinds of tongues*; to ***another*** the *interpretation of tongues* (1 Corinthians 12:10)

Notice the word God placed here ***to leave no question that "****diverse kinds of tongues****" is clearly separated as a different*** *Gift* ***as the "****Interpretation of Tongues****"***. The phrase "*to* ***another***" demands that "*Prayer Language*" is separated from the "*Interpreter*" as a unique "*another*" Believer. This is written as a *Command* that the Believer "Speaking In Tongues" *cannot* be the same Believer as the "Interpreter" but "***another***" Believer!

Without a Believer *Gifted* with the "*Interruption of Tongues*", it would leave the words of "*Tongues*" wholly *unverifiable*. This is a classic example of "Circular Reasoning"... Circular Reasoning paraphrased, "this is true, because I said its true, therefore its true".

This is the playground for the Devil to deceive the Children of GOD. Using Circular Reasoning defeats the whole *built-in checks-and-balances system* that GOD has as a *safeguard against human meddling and ignorance*. A *safeguard* ***keeping Believers safe behind the wall that GOD built***. Do not play on the edges... ***We all know what happened to Humpty Dumpty!***

I have observed many times where Believers were supposedly "*praying In tongues*" were waiting on an "*Interpretation*" to *verify* that the "*Tongues*" that they have *spoken* was from GOD. There is an overwhelming temptation among the over-zealous Believers, and ravenous wolves seeking vain-glory, to step in and play "God"!

*These try to **"Interpret"** their own **"word"**. **That is** not possible and Stands wholly against the Word of GOD!* It is *Biblically required* that the *Interpreter* be *another* Believer than the "*Speaker of Tongues*". *Not Today Satan, Not Today!*

We Cannot Compromise: No Interrupter, No Tongues...

If ***another*** Believer does not have an "*Interpretation of the Tongue*", then either the "*Tongue*" or the "*Interpreter*", or both, are *illegitimate*. *The devil spirit*[61] *that they are conjuring up is not the Holy Spirit!* This is a major example of how *confusion* can *creep into the Church unawares*.

Satan does his best work in the cracks and "gray" areas. (*There are no gray areas with GOD!* Any discoloring of GOD's pure luminescence is the venom of unadulterated false theology.) In this, "tongues" would be exposed as a Devil inspired false "*praying in tongues*".

---

[61] Beloved, believe not every spirit, but try the spirits whether they are of God: because many false prophets are gone out into the world. (1 John 4:1).

This makes the speaker of a false "tongues" rightly humiliated and condemned. In this, the Speaker of the purposed "tongue" cannot then confirm[62] their own "word". This is nothing more than the sin of *pride* and *self-righteousness* rearing its ugly head. It is an Impostor mocking God who can only be exposed using God's Legitimate "*Tongues Verification Method*"™© of the "*Interpretation of Tongues*".

Tongues Verification Method™©...

Accountability is paramount to God in His Gifting to Believers... After all, that is exactly what God is intending with "*Interpretation of Tongues*" is to *Guarantee* a legitimate "*Tongue*" and expose a *deceptive* "*praying in tongues*".

Intentional *Mis*interpretation and *Mis*information:
As mentioned, "*Tongues*", in most of the "legalistic" denominations, is dismissed out-of-hand, simply because they are *not comfortable with it*. This strikes me as a bit odd given that it is a *work* and *Gift of God the Holy Spirit*. The Holy Spirit is our *Guarantee* standing in the middle.

To dismiss ***Tongues*** *is to dismiss God's Power*

To dismiss Tongues is to dismiss God's Power in and through the Believer. This is a major reason that the Church has become Powerless! Is it any wonder then that *the Church has become more like the world, and much less like Heaven*?

[62] Yea, they have chosen their own ways, and their soul delighteth in their abominations. (Isaiah 66:3).

Seldom does anyone call out these conspirators, as few Believer's take the time to study the Scriptures as a Whole using *God's "Tongues Verification Method"*©™. These just *blindly* accept whatever they are told. (Do You Remember the 3 Blind Mice? Hint: the farmer's wife, Who cut off their tails with a carving knife!?) *Don't be a blind mice…*

The *Gift of Tongues* is _only_ Given by God the Holy Spirit to a *Selected* Group of Believers… _*not all Believers will get this Gift*_!
The "Gift" of Tongues is the least given Gift of the Holy Spirit:

> And God hath set some in the church, *first* apostles, secondarily prophets, thirdly teachers, *after that* miracles, then gifts of healings, helps, governments, *diversities of tongues*. (1 Corinthians 12:28).

As demonstrated above, "*Speaking in Tongues*" is the ***lowest*** *Gift on God's priority list*, equal in priority to the "*Interpretation of Tongues*".

These 2 Gifts *must always operate simultaneously and conjointly*. The "*Interpretation of Tongues*" operates only in conjunction with "*Speaking in Tongues*". The "*Interpretation of Tongues*" ties for *last place* making it very rare compared with the other Gifts of the Spirit:

> For to one is given by the [Holy] Spirit the word of wisdom; to another the word of knowledge by the same Spirit; To another faith by the same Spirit; to another the gifts of healing by the same Spirit; To another the working of miracles; to another prophecy; to another discerning of spirits; *to another divers kinds of* [*Speaking In*] *tongues*; *to another* ***the*** *interpretation of tongues*: (1 Corinthians 12:8-10)

Many from the More "*Legalistic-Bent*" Denominations Strive to Dismiss "Tongues" using this verse in its unGodly cherry-picked truncation:

> Charity [Godly love] never faileth: but whether there be prophecies, they shall fail; *whether there be tongues, they*

> *shall cease*; whether there be knowledge, it shall vanish away. (1 Corinthians 13:8)

In the verse above, the legalists cherry-pick "*tongues... shall cease*", while completely ignoring the surrounding context *in the same sentence, of the same verse!* Humm... if their *theology* is correct about this verse, then all "knowledge" must have also already "vanish[ed] away". While there is certainly a growing ignorance in the world today, knowledge still exists on planet earth. In the very least sense, the *Bible* tells us, ***Evil Makes You Stupid!***[63] (*Funny, Not Funny, but True!*)

As another inconvenient fact, the *Bible* prophesizes of the End Times that "*knowledge* shall be *increased*"[64]. So, clearly this verse is *not* talking about the "*Gift of Tongues*". Which according to the false cherry-pickers, should have *already* passed away.

I'm pretty sure that neither human "tongues", "language", nor "knowledge" have neither ceased, nor passed away. Cherry-pickers are *dangerous* **re**-*Writers* of God's Word. I do not think that that sits well with God ... The Judge of the damned... Just saying...

Beware of the Footnotes:

These rewriters and cherry-pickers of God's Word would say, "see *Tongues* was only temporary as it ceased after the establishment of the First Centaury Church". *Even the novice Christian can easily see that this verse in no way says that "Tongues", as in God's "Gift of Tongues", has ceased.* Tongues will cease when we reach Heaven, where I believe that only the Hebrew language will be spoken by the Saints. *No Interpretation necessary!*

---

[63] The Holy Bible: Psalms 107:17. See also Dr. el Yerak's Book: The Left's War Against God! and The Right's RULES FOR ANTI-RADICALS!: A Call To ACTION!; Volume 01; Master Level Edition; pg. 241.

[64] Daniel 12:4.

However, as theorized earlier in this Chapter, it seems that the Gift of "*Speaking In Tongues*" may be a *temporary* Gift for specific Believers, for specific times, for witnessing Salvation in Jesus. That would make the "Gift of Tongues" ***temporary*** in some Believer's life's, but operating continuously in the Church until the conclusion of the Church Age when the trumpet blows…

Always use ***God's Bible Puzzle Pieces* Study *Method***™ to sort the Devil's false "*praying in tongues*" *from God's blessed* "*Speaking In Tongues*".

Legalists attempt to lump "*Tongues*" together with several Gifts of the Holy Spirit and ***re-****Categorize [****re-****Version]* them as "sign gifts". (another "*tradition-of-men*" and Luciferian trick.[65]) This is in an attempt to disconnect their *man-created* category of "sign gifts" from other Gifts of the Spirit, from which they are not threatened.

This *theology* simply exists nowhere in the *Bible*. Keep an eye out for Cherry-pickers, "'*Bible*' critics", atheistic mythologists, and *Bible* destroyers. All those roads lead to a fiery Judgement.

These so-called "sign gifts" are generally identified as: *Speaking in Tongues*, the *Interpretation of Tongues*, healing, working miracles, and *prophesying*.

It is no coincidence that the Gifts of the Spirit, which the Powerless religionaires cast-off, are all the Holy Spirit *POWER* Gifts! In my "legalistically approved" study *Bible* footnotes, *Speaking In Tongues* is dismissed out-of-hand:

> Just as it is necessary to erect a scaffolding when a building is being erected, so sign gifts were spiritual scaffolding used by God to give credibility to His revelation which became the

[65] See the author's Book: El Yerak, Dr. Rhema; The Left's War Against God! and The Right's RULES FOR ANTI-RADICALS!: A Call To ACTION!; Volume 01; Master Level Edition; Chapter Bait and Switch: The Re-Name-Game: page 85 ff.

foundation of the church. When the written word of God was complete, God removed the scaffolding.

Wait… What? Of course, this terminology of using some made-up "scaffolding" is *man-made* and nowhere to be found in the *Bible*. But boy does it make these unlearned wannabes seem "*learned*"[66] in their *self-righteousness*! This is a prime example of the sinful "*traditions-of-men*" supplanting the actual "'*Commandments*'[67] of God"[68].[69]

ANYONE who Identifies themselves as a "Bible Critic"… Is NOT a Christian.

Some contrarywise Christians say this cherry-picked snippet "proves tongues ceased after the first Century Church was established". There are several Doctrinal problems with that statement…

First, the "*tongues*" here are existing human languages, *not* the *Gift of Tongues*. **Second**, those who promote this ***re***-*Writing [**re**-Versioning]* of God's Word, use only a truncated, comma delineated, cherry-picked, piece of a verse. Hummm… These same saboteurs are quick to point out "*cherry-picking*" is what *cults* and *wayward "Christianity"* promotes… Get the beam out of thine own eye![70]

---

[66] Beware lest any man spoil you through philosophy and vain deceit, after the tradition of men, after the rudiments of the world, and not after Christ (Colossians 2:8).

[67] For "Commanded" see chapter: Believers Commanded to Use Prayer Language!

[68] Matthew 15:9; 1 Timothy 4:1.

[69] See authors books: el Yerak, Dr Rhema; WALKING BY FAITH… What Is Faith, How To Live By Faith, and Finally Living the Victorious Christian Life!; Advanced Level Edition; and el Yerak, Dr Rhema; The Left's War Against God! and The Right's RULES FOR ANTI-RADICALS!: A Call To ACTION! Volume 01; Master Level Edition.

[70] Matthew 7:3-5.

If your *Puzzle* doesn't work, then you have *erred*, and ***your*** *theology must be corrected*. ***To stay right with God, you must tear apart your errant puzzle, and begin again, and again if necessary, until all pieces fit flawlessly together.***

Tear It Apart and Start... *Again*!

Legalists are otherwise hyper-vigilant about not "cherry-picking" Scriptures. They are quick to point out this error in other denominations and cults, and rightfully identifying them as heretical. Yet somehow, they themselves see no conflict cherry-picking this verse. They take it wholly out of context, without any thought of self-application of their own anti-cherry-picking *Bible* *theology*. Cherry-picked *theology* ***always*** leads to theological and Doctrinal *corruption*. This is a convenient ***per-****Version* on their part. Do as they say, not as they do...

Either all of the Bible works together, or the Bible doesn't work at all.

This is why God *Commands* Believers to "*compare-spiritual-to-spiritual*" and *NOT* "*compare spiritual with the traditions-of-men*". This "footnote heresy" is repeated over-and-over in the footnotes throughout my legalistic "study" *Bible*. Satan is very clever indeed...

Ignorance is No Excuse:

Believers *cannot* hide behind an excuse of "but I didn't know". God specifically tells us that "*ignorance* is *no excuse*" before God:

> When a ruler hath sinned, and done somewhat through *ignorance* against any of the commandments of the LORD [JEHOVAH] his God concerning things which should not be done, *and is guilty*; (Leviticus 4:22)
>
> And if a soul sin, and commit any of these things which are forbidden to be done by the commandments of the LORD [JEHOVAH]; *though he wist* [*knew*] *it not, yet is he guilty*, and *shall bear his iniquity*.[71] (Leviticus 5:17)

I myself was grossly misled for decades by preachers depriving me of a vibrant and deep relationship with GOD. This was my, albeit temporary, excuse for my ignorance of GOD's Doctrine on "*praying in tongues*".

However, in my ruminating, GOD tapped me on my shoulder, as He often does, and whispered in my ear, "Yes but you could have read it in the *Bible* for yourself all along ". Humm... Oops... Checked by GOD again... I am grateful for the patience and kindness of GOD.

Be open to letting GOD... *be GOD*. Growing includes allowing GOD to purify and purge our faults and theology... Purifying, purging, and going through the refiner's fire hurts and humbles the Believer!:

> But who may abide the day of his coming? and who shall stand when he appeareth? for he is like a refiner's fire, and like fullers' soap: (Malachi 3:2).

My ignorance was, and is, my own fault. (son of a goatherders mother, I hate it when that happens.) The *reckless and misleading clergy will answer for their own sins*, but I will have to answer for mine. *Taking personal responsibility is not always as easy as you might think...*

---

[71] For "Iniquity" see Rhéma el Yerak's upcoming Book: *Curses and Christians: What Does GOD Say?*.

The "Church" is in an *ongoing* state of construction by the Holy Spirit. This Construction which will not end until the Church is taken out of the world with the indwelling Holy Spirit at the Rapture.[72] The *Bible* Canon is complete, but the Church's construction is still *ongoing*...

GOD is Sure to Hyper-*Emphasize* that *No One* Has the Excuse of Forbidding to Speak with Tongues:

> Wherefore, brethren, covet to prophesy, and
> ***forbid not to speak with tongues***. (1 Corinthians 14:39)

"*Prayer Language*" becomes unnecessarily frightening when it is *falsely labeled* "*praying in tongues*". Chaos only exists in Evil. JESUS, the Face[73] of GOD, is *Simple*. Evil is *subtile*, *corrupt*, and *built on Lies!*[74] Choose ye this day whom ye will serve...[75] *Serving GOD is always Simple, but not necessarily always Easy...*

There can be no "Speaking In Tongues" without a corresponding "Interpretation of Tongues".

As discussed, I have experienced many, many times where a person is claiming to be "Speaking in Tongues" and there was no one there to "Interpret" it as a discernable human language, you know, the whole "Tongue" part.

[72] For the mystery of iniquity doth already work: only he who now letteth will let, until he be taken out of the way. And then shall that Wicked be revealed, whom the Lord shall consume with the spirit of his mouth, and shall destroy with the brightness of his coming: Even him, whose coming is after the working of Satan with all power and signs and lying wonders, And with all deceivableness of unrighteousness in them that perish; because they received not the love of the truth, that they might be saved. (2 Thessalonians 2:7-10).

[73] For God, who commanded the light to shine out of darkness, hath shined in our hearts, to give the light of the knowledge of the glory of *God in the face of Jesus Christ*." (2 Corinthians 4:6).

[74] 2 Corinthians 11:3.

[75] Joshua 24:15.

An *Interpreter of Tongues* is *required* by GOD to come alongside of a "*Tongue*" and "*Interpret*" the Believer's "*Tongue*". This is a *Commandment* of GOD to ***ensure*** that the person is "Speaking in Tongues", and *not speaking from demonic spirit*[76]. GOD has *built-in checks-and-balances* of the "*Interpretation of Tongues*" to *ensure* GOD's intended result in His faithful Church!

There can be *no "Speaking In Tongues" without a corresponding* "*Interpretation of Tongues*". You have to appreciate GOD's foresight and understanding of Believers' collective weaknesses!

[76] Beloved, believe not every spirit, but try the spirits whether they are of God: because many false prophets are gone out into the world. (1 John 4:1).

04. The Gifts of the Spirit Are NOT for Every Believer:

The Gift of Tongues...

The *Gift* of "*Speaking In Tongues*" is an exclusive "*Gift*" from the Holy Spirit for those so *Elected*.[77] Believers are *Gifted only* for a very specific reason, a specific time, and for witnessing Salvation to unbelievers:

> And *when the day of Pentecost was fully come*, they were all with one accord in one place. And suddenly there came a sound from heaven as of a rushing mighty wind, and it filled all the house where they were sitting. *And there appeared unto them cloven tongues like as of fire, and it sat upon each of them.* And they were *all filled with the Holy Ghost* [Spirit] and began to *speak with other tongues*, as the [Holy] *Spirit gave them utterance* [spoke through them]. (Acts 2:1-4)

The Day of Pentecost the ***Gift*** of Tongues Given

The First New Testament Day of Pentecost:

On the Day of the first New Testament Pentecost, the *flaming* "*TONGUES*" were a manifestation of the Holy Spirit to witness Jesus, in the newly given, New Testament Salvation...

[77] Hebrews 2:4.

John the Baptist Prophesied the first giving of a Believer's Prayer Language:

> John answered, saying unto *them* all, I indeed baptize you with water; but one mightier than I cometh, the latchet of whose shoes I am not worthy to unloose: *he* [JESUS] *shall baptize you with the Holy Ghost and with fire*: (Luke 3:16)

Speaking In Tongues is the Exclusive Manifestation of the Holy Spirit:
There is a significance in the Holy Spirit manifesting as *Flaming "Tongues"*. *Fire* in the *Bible*, is often symbolic of the *presence* and *Power* of the *Holy Spirit*.[78] *The Holy Spirit is the Power of the Tongue of GOD*.

> And they were all *filled with the Holy Ghost*, and began to speak with other ***tongues***, as the [Holy] Spirit gave them utterance. (Acts 2:4)

> And when Paul had laid his hands upon them, the *Holy Ghost came on them*; and they *spake with* ***tongues***, and prophesied. (Acts 19:6)

Speaking in Tongues is *Only* for Witnessing JESUS to *Unbelievers*; and *Praying In the Spirit* is *Only for the Believer*:

> Wherefore ***tongues*** *are for a* ***sign***, not to them that believe, but *to* ***them that believe not***: but prophesying serveth not for them that believe not, but for *them which* ***believe***. (1 Corinthians 14:22)

Speaking in Tongues is for the *Entire* Church Age:
GOD's "Will" has not changed as it is impossible for GOD to change:[79]

> And there are diversities of operations, but it is the same God

[78] I indeed baptize you with water unto repentance: but he that cometh after me is mightier than I, whose shoes I am not worthy to bear: he shall baptize you with the Holy Ghost, and with fire: (Matthew 3:11).
[79] Hebrews 13:8; Malachi 3:6; *et al.*

> which worketh all in all. But *the **manifestation** of the* [Holy] *Spirit* is *given to every man to* ***profit withal*** [all the Body]. For *to one is given by the [Holy] Spirit* the word of wisdom; to another the word of knowledge by the same Spirit; To another faith by the same Spirit; to another the gifts of healing by the same Spirit; To another the working of miracles; to another prophecy; to another discerning of spirits; to ***another*** *divers* [*different*] *kinds of tongues*; *to* ***another*** the *interpretation of tongues*: But all these worketh that one and the selfsame Spirit, ***dividing*** *to every man severally as he [the Spirit] will*. For as the body is one, and hath many members, and all the members of that one body, being many, are one body: so also is Christ. (1 Corinthians 12:6-12)

Every Believer is *given at least one Gift of the Holy Spirit*.
What is your Gift or Gifts? It is essential that we engage God to discover our Gift(s). Our Gift is a Gift that feels absolutely natural, like you were born to exercise the Gift. ***It is your God-driven Purpose!*** My primary Gift is being a Master[80] Teacher including writing, teaching Discipleship, and hands-on Ministry. When I fall into the flow of the Holy Spirit through me, *all is well with my soul.* ***Purpose*** drives your soul. Find your Gift. Again, your Gift(s) will feel like you were born to do it! You will instinctively know it in your spirit when you find it. Go God!

Once you have discovered your Gift(s) follow up in the Scriptures using ***God's Perfect Bible Puzzle Study Method*** to discover the outworkings and limits of your Gift. God Bless you on your Journey in Growing with God, effecting others for Christ Jesus, and becoming the ***Purpose*** you were born to accomplish for Eternity!

The "*Gift*" of Tongues is only *Given* by the Will of the Father, Empowered by the Holy Spirit, and Authorized in Jesus' name… to

[80] My brethren, be not many masters, knowing that we shall receive the greater condemnation. (James 3:1).

Select Believers... *not all* Believers![81]

The "Gift" of "*Speaking In Tongues*" is the ***Least*** given Gift of the Holy Spirit:

> And God hath set some in the church, *first* apostles, *secondarily* prophets, *thirdly* teachers, *after that* miracles, then gifts of healings, helps, governments, [and ***lastly***] *diversities of tongues*. (1 Corinthians 12:28).

The "Gift" of the Manifestation of "*Speaking In Tongues*" Began in the New Testament when the Holy Spirit First Fell *upon* Believers:

> While Peter yet spake these words, *the Holy Ghost fell on all them* which heard the word. And they of the circumcision which believed were astonished, as many as came with Peter, because that on the Gentiles also was poured out *the gift of the Holy Ghost*. For they heard them *speak with tongues* [existing human languages], and magnify God. Then answered Peter, (Acts 10:44-46).

Speaking In Tongues is the Lowest Gift on GOD's Gifting Priority Scale:

[81] Again, The "*Gift*" of *Speaking In Tongues* is selected as an exclusive Gift only for a *Select* few as chosen by the Holy Spirit. Whereas *Prayer Language* and *Praying In the Spirit*, are available to *ALL* Believers. See especially the following chapter: *Prayer Language: Is It Biblical?*.

Speaking In Tongues is to Speak to Those Who believe *not*, in Their own Native Tongue, to Praise God and Witness Jesus for Salvation.

> Wherefore *tongues are for a sign*, not to them that believe, but *to them that believe not*: but prophesying serveth not for them that believe not, but for them which believe (1 Corinthians 14:22).

The definition of the "Gifts" of the Spirit becomes enlivened in the Believer when using: ***God's Perfect Bible Puzzle Study Method***™ and in God's Foundation of "*comparing-spiritual-to-spiritual*".

By recognizing the, not so nuanced, differences in Scripture, we can clearly see the Truth when comparing verses-to-verses[82]. Every Believer has at least one of the Gifts of the Holy Spirit, assigned as God needs Believers to have the Gift(s).

...It's All About God!

[82] God's comparing spiritual to spiritual is the foundation upon which ***God's Perfect Bible Puzzle Study Method***™ is built and stands.

Book Notes

05. *Prayer Language: Is It Biblical?*

The Holy Spirit Speaks…

The Most Important Question Surrounding *Prayer Language* is…

"Is It Biblical?".

We will build on the following, and *other* verses, that clearly teach *"Praying In the Spirit"* is ***Biblical***… and even ***Commanded by GOD***. *Praying In the Spirit* is the *Power* that holds the **Believer's Armor of GOD** together, and ***Empowers*** the Believer in ***Spiritual Warfare***. According to GOD's Word, ***Victorious Spiritual Warfare*** is *ONLY* possible when exercising *Prayer Language*.[83] It brings the Holy Spirit directly into Battle!

Here is a partial list of *Bible* references that you can look up where *Praying In the Spirit* is exemplified for *all* Believers:

- Acts 2:3
- Romans 8:26
- Ephesians 6:18
- 1 Corinthians 14:2
- 1 Corinthians 14:4
- 1 Corinthians 14:14
- 1 Corinthians 14:15
- 1 Corinthians 14:16
- 1 Corinthians 14:18
- 1 Corinthians 14:39
- Jude 1:20

[83] See especially the chapter: Prayer Language: the Missing Power In the Armor of GOD.

Again, ALL Believers have access to their GODly: *Prayer Language*.

In contrast to the small numbers of those Believers who receive the Gift of Tongues, *ALL Believers have access to their unique and GODly Prayer Language.*

Prayer Language ***is what GOD uses through Believers when we*** *Pray In the Spirit*. (As, a ***Tracking Reminder,*** *Prayer Language* is the *noun* form, and *Praying In the Spirit* is the *verb* form.[84])

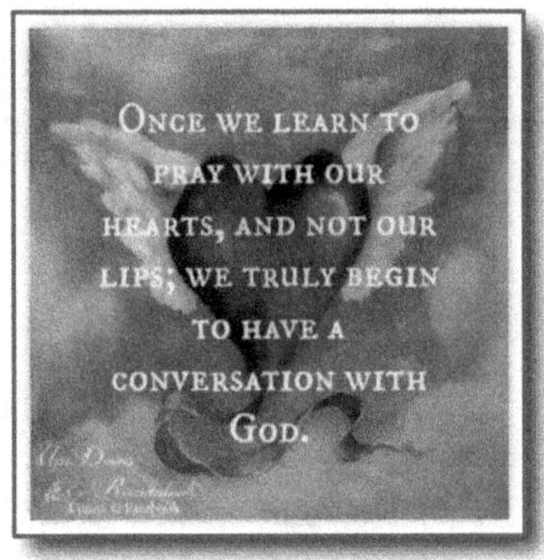

Praying In the Spirit is *Empowered* by GOD

The distinction that separates the *Gift of Tongues* from *Prayer Language* is that "*Prayer Language*" *is for all Believers* given to the Believer from GOD. "*Speaking In Tongues*" *is only for a selected few Believers* as chosen by the Holy Spirit, as GOD wills it.[85]

Prayer Language is *GOD's unique*, humanly unintelligible, and sypher encoded *Language of GOD*. This is the *Language* that God the Holy Spirit carries through the conduit of the Believer's heart... *to the Father's Ears! Prayer Language* is not a series of disjointed and meaningless syllables of manmade gibberish. *Prayer Language*, like

[84] ("*Speaking In Tongues*" is the *verb* form; and "*Tongues*" is the *noun* form.)
[85] 1 Corinthians 12:7-11.

all languages, it *flows with an innate rhythm and cadence* with only a few repetitive words[86]. ***Again Recall…*** *Prayer Language is a literal Language of GOD*.

Believers Pray Directly to the Father on the Throne

Prayer Language is unique to the New Testament with the giving of the indwelling of the Holy Spirit in the Believer's spirit. There are no Old Testament references to a Believer's *Prayer Language*, and by definition, there cannot be.

Prayer Language is a literal… Language of GOD.

When I *Pray In the Spirit*, GOD reveals His thoughts to me. This is essential when *Praying* over people for things like Healing, Words of Wisdom, and Words of Knowledge.

From Our Lips… to GOD's Ears.

JESUS No Longer Prays to the Father for Believers:

In the New Testament, it is the Person of the Holy Spirit Who Carries our Prayers to the Father on the Throne of GOD:

> And in that day ***ye shall ask me nothing***. Verily, verily, I say unto you, Whatsoever ye shall ***ask the Father in my name***… *I*

[86] See upcoming chapter: *The ShaNaNa Delusion*.

*say **not** unto you, that I will pray the Father for you*: (John 16:23-26)

JESUS said "I say ***not*** unto you, that I will *pray the Father for you*"... If JESUS isn't praying to the Father, Who then will carry our Prayers to the Father on the Throne of GOD? The Father cannot pray to Himself. And JESUS stands next to the Father on His Throne in Heaven. That leaves only one Person of the GODhead[87]... the Holy Spirit!

JESUS No Longer Prays to the Father for Us!

Tongues Requires 2 to 3 Believers...
The name of JESUS is the *Authority* by which Believers' Prayers are *Authenticated*. If there is *No Authority* in the name of JESUS, then *No prayers* reach The Father Who is the "Will" of GOD. This *Authentication* is facilitated by the Seal[88] in JESUS' name as *Empowered* and *Enacted* by the *Holy Spirit*.

Prayer Language is ***GOD's*** unique and sypher encoded Languages that God the Holy Spirit carries through the conduit of the Believer's heart (spirit) and mouth, to the ears of God the Father on The Throne in Heaven, *in the name of JESUS*. Without the Believer's sealing their prayers in the Authority *of* JESUS' name, the Holy Spirit is helpless to carry our Prayers to the Throne.

Praying In the Spirit:
Believers *cannot* self-will the Gifts of the Holy Spirit upon themselves,

[87] el Yerak, Dr Rhema, *The Trinity of GOD; The GODhead*: *What Does GOD say?;* Acts 17:29, Romans 1:20, and Colossians 2:9.

[88] In whom ye also trusted, after that ye heard the word of truth, the gospel of your salvation: in whom also after that ye believed, ye were *sealed with that holy Spirit* of promise, (Ephesians 1:13).

nor anyone else for that matter. This is a self-righteous[89] attempt… a fool's errand[90] in *trying to usurp God!* ***In review***, *Praying In the Spirit* is for *EVERY* Believer, and the *Gift of Tongues* is only for a small number of Christians to whom the Holy Spirit specifically wills it to be so[91].

Praying In the Spirit is for ***all*** Believers:

> *Praying always* with all prayer and supplication *in the* [Holy] *Spirit*, and watching thereunto with all perseverance and supplication *for **all** saints*; (Ephesians 6:18).

Prayer Language is an Amazing spiritual *Empowerment* from the Holy Spirit Equipping ***all*** the Saints. *Praying In the Spirit* is absolutely essential to *Empower* ***every*** Believer in *Spiritual Warfare*:

Praying In the Spirit…

- **1.** *Praying In the Spirit* is *Personal*!
- **2.** *Praying In the Spirit* is *not* for *Corporate* or Church Assembly Praying!
- **3.** *Praying In the Spirit* is *only between you and God*.
- **4.** *Praying In the Spirit* *Empowers* ("builds up") the *individual* Believer *for War*.
- **5.** *Praying In the Spirit* is *God's unique* and sypher encoded *Language*.
- **6.** *Praying In the Spirit* The *Spoken Rhema* Language *Releases the Power* of Praying In the Spirit.

---

[89] Isaiah 64:6.
[90] Acts 8:18-21.
[91] 1 Corinthians 12:11.

Let's flesh this out:

✝ **1.** *Praying In the Spirit* is *Personal*

Praying In the Spirit Empowers the Individual Believer: *Praying In the Spirit* draws the Believer's heart closer to GOD. *Praying In the Spirit* opens the Believer's spiritual ears and eyes to see what GOD hears, sees, and says in what GOD is revealing to us.

Praying In the Spirit often imparts *Words of Wisdom*[92] and *Words of Knowledge*[93] to the person *Praying*. These words are Imparted through the Believer when we Pray over a person. Thereby allowing Believers to speak GOD's Words *into* the unsaved, and Believer's lives as well.

Praying In the Spirit is Personal

✝ **2.** *Praying In the Spirit* is NOT Corporate/Public Prayer.

Praying In the Spirit is only from the Believer's heart to GOD's ears. *From our lips... to GOD's ears* as facilitated by the Spirit.

✝ **3.** *Praying In the Spirit* is only between you and GOD.

When we speak into a person's life something that only GOD knows, the person knows it's not from us, but a Word from GOD. *Praying In the Spirit edifies the individual Believer* and vicariously those whom

92 See Dr el Yerak's upcoming Book: el Yerak, Dr Rhema; *Gifts of the Spirit: What Does GOD Say?*

93 For to one is given by the Spirit the *word of wisdom*; to *another the word of knowledge* by the same Spirit; (1 Corinthians 12:8).

we are Praying:

> For he that speaketh in an unknown tongue *speaketh* [prays] *not unto men, but unto God: for no man **understandeth** him*; howbeit in the [Holy] [S]pirit he *speaketh mysteries*... He that speaketh in an unknown tongue *edifieth himself*; but he that prophesieth edifieth the church. (1 Corinthians 14:4)

✝ **4**. *Praying In the Spirit* Builds-Up [*Empowers* and *Encourages*] the Believer for War:

> But ye, beloved, *building up yourselves* on your most holy faith, *praying in the Holy Ghost* [Holy Spirit], (Jude 1:20).

✝ **5**. *Praying In the Spirit* is *God's* unique, encoded Godly Language:

No person, nor angel can understand the Languages of God. This is one reason why "*Prayer Language*" is ***un***reconcilably disconnected from "*Speaking in Tongues*", and by extension the *Gift of* "*Interpretation of Tongues*" which is also ***in***compatible with a Believer's *Prayer Language*:

> For *he that **speaketh** in an **unknown tongue** speaketh not unto men, **but unto God**: for no man understandeth him*; howbeit in the spirit he speaketh *mysteries*. (1 Corinthians 14:2)

A *Tracking* Reminder™©[94]

"*Speaking* in Tongues" is a Believer *Speaking to Unbelievers*

"*Praying* In the Spirit" is a Believer *Praying to God*.

As such, this encoded Language of God also makes it *impossible* for demons to understand. This allows the Believer to *privately* communicate to the Father *without any eavesdropping from devils*.

[94] *Subject Tracking Boxes* are ™ and © by Third Awakening Foundation Inc.

✝ 6. *Praying In the Spirit* The <u>*Spoken*</u> <u>*Rhema*</u> Language <u>*Releases the Power*</u> of *Praying In the Spirit*.

The word "word" in the New Testament is translated from two different *Kone*[95] *Greek* words which the original New Testament was written: the "<u>*Rhema*</u>" Word, which is the <u>*spoken*</u> *out-loud* Word, and the "<u>*Logos*</u>" Word as the <u>*written*</u> Word. Jesus is the *Logos* and *the Holy Spirit is the Power of the spoken "Rhema" Word*.

A *Believer must Pray* <u>*out-loud*</u> *to be Praying In the Spirit*. This is the *spoken out-loud* ***Rhema*** *Word* that releases the *Power* of the Holy Spirit.

The *Spoken* ***Rhema*** *Word* of God is *Empowered* by the Holy Spirit. God the Holy Spirit is the manifest *Presence* and *Power* of God:

> Now the God of hope fill you with all joy and peace in believing, that ye may abound in hope, *through the **power** of the **Holy Ghost***. (Romans 15:13)

Perhaps the most illustrative *Biblical* reference to the "moving of the Holy Spirit" is in Creation[96]. The Father *willed* it to be so, Jesus *spoke* the Word, and the Holy Spirit *exploded* Creation into existence… and "it was good".

God's *Rhema* Empowered Words are *Laying In-Wait…*

God's *Rhema* Empowered Words are *Laying In-Wait* in the Believer's spirit; Waiting to be *Spoken* and the *Latent Power* of God Released by the Holy Spirit…

> If ye abide ***in me***, and ***my words*** [*Rhema*] **abide *in you***, *ye shall ask* [<u>*speak*</u> the *Rhema* Words] what ye will, and it shall be done unto you. (John 15:7)

---

[95] The *New Testament* was originally written in *Kone Greek*. *Kone Greek* is considered a "dead language" as it is no longer used. *Kone Greek* is only kept "alive" as the foundation of the *Received Text Bible*. The only verification and dictionary of Kone Greek is from within the *Received Text Bible*.

[96] Genesis 1:2-3; See also upcoming chapter: *Ephesians Chapter 6: Spiritual* <u>*Warfare*</u>

> Now faith is the *substance* [*Latent Power waiting*] of things hoped for, *the evidence of things not seen*. (Hebrews 11:1)

---

*The Rhema Empowered Words **build Strength** and **lay in wait** as we **prepare for Battle, in Ever Increasing Latent Power,** as the growing, but as yet unreleased **Power of God**.*

Here is a New Testament Confirmation of the *Spoken Rhema Word*:

> In the beginning was **the** *Word* [*Logos*/Jesus the Christ v. 17], and the *Word* [*Logos*/Jesus] was with God, and the *Word* [*Logos*/Jesus] was God. *The same was in the beginning with God. All things were made by him; and without him was not any thing made that was made.* In him was life; and the life was the light of men. And the light shineth in darkness; and the darkness comprehended it not. (John 1:1-5)

Yes, the use of the Believer's *Prayer Language* is still a *Command*[97] of God:

> And take [a *Command* of God]... the sword of the *Spirit*, which is the *word* [*Rhema: spoken in Power*] of God: *Praying always with all prayer and supplication in the Spirit*, and watching [*building Latent Power*] thereunto with all [*Latent*] perseverance and supplication for all saints; (Ephesians 6:17-18)

Prayer Language is the primary and indispensable *Weapon* for all Believers. *All the Power in the Armor of God is the Spoken Rhema Word releasing the Holy Spirit.* The *spoken Rhema word* by God the Holy Spirit *literally connects together and Empowers all the pieces of our Armor of God.*

---

[97] For Prayer Language see chapter 12. Believers Commanded by God to Use Their Prayer Language!.

If you *don't* feel the *Power* of the Holy Spirit *surging* through you as a Believer, then you must allow the Holy Spirit to awaken your *Latent Power* waiting to be released through your *Prayer Language* which surges through you *and latently waits to be Released!...*

God is Either God of your all...

...or not your God at all.

06. Prayer Language and Spiritual Warfare:

The Empowered Warrior!

Is your *Spiritual Warfare* lacking the *Power* of GOD to *Empower* and *Encourage*[98] you to Victory? There is a really good *Biblical* reason for that… The following is a *Biblical* teaching for Believers on how to *surrender* to the work of the indwelling Holy Spirit. Believers must *Surrender* to become the *conduit* of the Holy Spirit to utilize the Latent *Power* of the *Believer's Spiritual Warfare*.

The Armor of GOD, Spiritual *Warfare*, and *Prayer Language*:

> Finally, my *brethren, be strong in the Lord, and in the power of his might*. Put on the whole armour of God, that ye may be able to stand against the wiles of the devil. For we wrestle not against flesh and blood, but against principalities, against powers, against the rulers of the darkness of this world, against spiritual wickedness in high places. Wherefore take unto you the whole armour of God, that ye may be able to withstand in the evil day, and having done all, to stand. Stand therefore, having your loins girt about with truth, and having

[98] For a much more in depth discussion GOD's Encouragement through Faith see author's Book: el Yerak, Dr Rhema; WALKING BY FAITH… What Is Faith, How To Live By Faith, and Finally Living the Victorious Christian Life!; Advanced Level Edition.

on the breastplate of righteousness; And your feet shod with the preparation of the gospel of peace; Above all [covering all], taking the shield of faith, wherewith ye shall be able to quench all the fiery darts of the wicked. And take the helmet of salvation, and the sword of the Spirit, which is the word of God: *Praying always* [***Prayer Language***] with all *prayer and supplication in the* ***[Holy]*** *Spirit*, and watching thereunto with all perseverance and supplication *for all saints*; And for me, that *utterance* [*Speaking In Tongues*] may be given unto me, that *I may open my mouth boldly, to make known the mystery of the gospel*, For which I am an ambassador in bonds: that therein I may speak boldly, *as I ought to speak*. [*Rhema* Word] (Ephesians 6:10-20)

This Scripture Passage is detailing the *Armor of God*, the whatfors and whynots, so to speak. It starts by giving us the *purpose* of the Armor of God, which is "*be strong in the Lord, and in the power of his might*". *A Believer's "Strength" is the Holy Spirit's "Power".* What is the *ONLY* way in which Believers become the *conduit* of the *Power* of God? This is answered in the conclusion of this chapter with the *Power* that enables the Believer to operate in all the adjoined pieces of the Armor of God...

Satan has been all too successful in blinding the eyes of Believers to the most important and indispensable *Weapon of our Spiritual Warfare*... our *Prayer Language*! Is it any wonder then, that Christians lack the *Power* of God in *Spiritual Warfare*? The devils know the rules... Do You?

The Armor of God is *useless, Powerless,* just an interesting flannelgraph story for children, and simply will *not* work *without Praying In the Spirit*[99]. *In the flannelgraph depiction below, there is no Power nor Legitimacy without the Holy Spirit*:

[99] Ephesians 6:17-18.

> ...and the *sword of the Spirit*, which is the [*Rhema* Spoken] word of God: *Praying always* with all prayer and supplication *in the Spirit*... (Ephesians 6:17b-18a).

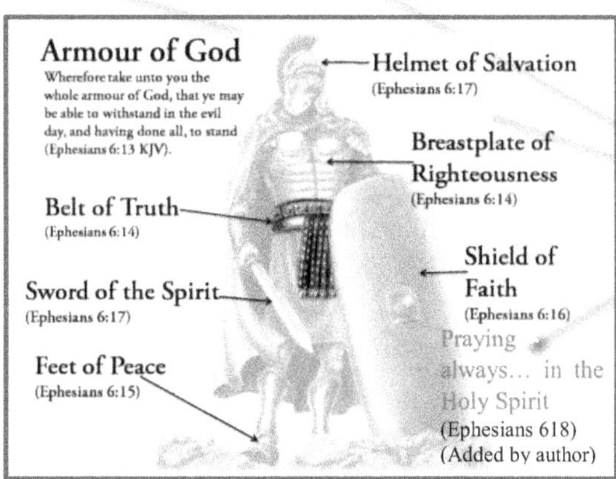

The Armor of GOD! ...well *almost* all of it...

Here are the Believers' *Biblically* Prescribed *Weapons of War* in *Spiritual Warfare* as *Activated* by the Holy Spirit Using Your *Prayer Language*. The intentional absence and ***per-***Version of the most important piece of the Armor of GOD in the *Praying In the Spirit*.

Praying In the Spirit is shrouded by Satan and his Luciferian minions such as, Westcott, Hort, Strong, and Blavatsky,[100]. So, let's just *add Praying always... in the Holy Spirit* back onto the flannelgraph to correctly reflect what the Word of GOD *actually* says.

This missing Piece of Armor is not an oversight, but a deliberate Legalistic sabotage. The Legalists do not like the Command of *Praying In the Spirit* so they erase it! *GOD help them!*

Not Today Satan... Not Today!

[100] See upcoming chapter: Appendix 2. The devils Doing the Devil's Work...; and Appendix 17: The "Westcott & Hort Only" Controversy...

Let's Explore the Practical Application of *Praying In the Spirit*:

- *Prayer Language* the Power that Holds the Armor of GOD Together.
- An Outward Demonstration that *Prayer Language* is of GOD.
- Supernatural Boldness.
- Healing.
- Signs and Wonders.
- Exorcism/Deliverance, the *Power* of GOD.
- Holy Spirit *Power* for Witnessing.
- Holy Spirit *Power*.
- Ministering.
- Christian Walk.
- Relationship with GOD.
- Special GODly Wisdom.
- A Sign of the Presence of GOD.

The Fully Dressed Warrior of GOD

Praying In the Spirit Detailed:

- Prayer Language the *Power* that Holds the Armor of GOD Together:

> ***Praying always*** **with all prayer and** ***supplication*** **in the** *[Holy]* ***Spirit***, and watching thereunto with all perseverance and supplication for all saints; (Ephesians 6:18)

The *Power* of Our Armor *IS* the *Power* of the Holy Spirit

† *Prayer Language* is a "<u>*Demonstration*</u>" that *Prayer Language* is of the *Power* of GOD

Being <u>*Spoken*</u> by the <u>*Holy Spirit*</u>:

> And my speech [*Rhema words*] and my preaching was not with enticing words of man's wisdom, but in *demonstration of the [Holy] Spirit* and of *power*... But we ***speak*** [*Rhema Word of Power*] the wisdom of God ***in a*** *mystery*, even the *hidden wisdom*, which God ordained before the world unto our glory: (1 Corinthians 2:4, 7).

† Supernatural *Boldness* to Preach Salvation in JESUS Christ:

> And when they had *prayed*, the place was shaken where they were assembled together; and they were all filled with the Holy Ghost, and they spake the word of God with *boldness*. (Acts 4:31)

† Healing, Signs, and Wonders:

> By stretching forth thine hand to *heal*; and that *signs* and *wonders* may be done by the name of thy holy child Jesus. (Acts 4:30)

✝ Exorcism/Deliverance, the Power of God for:

> How God *anointed* Jesus of Nazareth *with the Holy Ghost* and with *power*: who went about doing good, and ***healing** all that were **oppressed of the devil***; for God was with him (Acts 10:38)

✝ Holy Spirit *Power* for Witnessing:

> But *ye shall receive **power**, after that the Holy Ghost is come upon you*: and ye shall be ***witnesses*** unto me both in Jerusalem, and in all Judaea, and in Samaria, and unto the uttermost part of the earth. (Acts 1:8)

✝ Holy Spirit *Power*:

> For our gospel came not unto you in [written *Logos*] word only, but also in *power [of the spoken Rhema Word]*, and *in the Holy Ghost*, and in much assurance; as ye know what manner of men we were among you for your sake. (1 Thessalonians 1:5)

✝ Ministering and the Christian Walk:

> Who also declared unto us *your love in the [Holy] Spirit*. For this cause we also, since the day we heard it, do not cease to pray for you, and to desire that *ye might be filled with the knowledge of his will in all wisdom and spiritual understanding*; That ye might *walk worthy* of the Lord unto all pleasing, *being **fruitful** in every good work*, and *increasing in the **knowledge** of God*; ***Strengthened** with all **might***, according to his glorious *power*, unto all patience and longsuffering with joyfulness; (Colossians 1:8-11)

✝ Special Wisdom:

In addition to the previous verse set, here is more Spiritual Wisdom:

> *Praying always* with all ***prayer** and supplication in the [Holy] Spirit*, and *watching thereunto with all perseverance and*

> *supplication for all saints*; And for me, that *utterance may be given unto me*, that *I may open my mouth boldly* [*Rhema* Words], *to make known the mystery of the gospel*, For which I am an ambassador in bonds: that therein I may speak ***boldly**, as I ought to speak* [*Rhema* Words]. (Ephesians 6:18-20)

Praying In the Spirit is the Lifeblood of the ***Power***, Cohesion, Wisdom, and Opportunity of.

✝ **A** Sign of the Presence of God: *Victorious Spiritual Warfare*

> Fight the good fight of faith, lay hold on eternal life, whereunto thou art also called, and *hast professed [spoken Rhema* Word] a good profession before many witnesses. (1 Timothy 6:12)

The Holy Spirit...

Prayer Language comes by the Holy Spirit, through the heart of the Believer, and *not from the Believer's conscious mind*. *Prayer Language* is remarkably helpful *when the Believer does not know what to pray, or even how to pray.*

> Likewise the Spirit also helpeth our infirmities: *for we know not what we should pray* for as we ought: but *the* [*Holy*] ***Spirit** itself maketh **intercession** [Prayer Language] for us with **groanings** which cannot be uttered [Prayer Language]*. (Romans 8:26)

Half the Battle:

Half of *Spiritual Warfare* is remaining fully surrendered to the Holy Spirit, day-by-day, and keep our biases, and lusts out of the equation.[101] Half of our *Spiritual Warfare* is spent fighting *our* own sinful flesh and giving it up to God. We must remain surrendered to

---

[101] This I say then, Walk in the Spirit, and ye shall not fulfil the lust of the flesh. For the flesh lusteth against the Spirit, and the Spirit against the flesh: and these are contrary the one to the other: so that ye cannot do the things that ye would. (Galatians 5:16-17).

the Holy Spirit in GOD's *Agape* Love.

Only By the Holy Spirit

A Tracking Note: *Praying In the Spirit Cannot* Be Spoken Without the Holy Spirit: *Prayer Language* is *meaningless*, in fact, it's *not Prayer Language* at all, unless the Holy Spirit is *DIRECTLY* originating, speaking, *Empowering*, guiding, delivering, and encoding a Believer's *Prayer Language*.

Again, for Tracking Cohesion: When the Holy Spirit is not the originator of "*Prayer Language*", then it is *NOT Prayer* Language. It's *nonsense* that creates the *chaos* and *confusion* as characterized by the Apostle Paul. This chaos and confusion are what you feel in a room of pretenders and imposters "*praying in tongues*".

> Else when thou shalt bless with the [by the Holy] [S]pirit, how shall he that occupieth the room of the unlearned say Amen at thy giving of thanks, seeing he understandeth not what thou *sayest* [*Rhema Words*]? (1 Corinthians 14:16)

This is why in the middle of Paul's instruction on the isolation between the "*Gift of Tongues*" and "*Praying In the Spirit*", Paul stops to warn Believers of the Devil's *mocking "praying in tongues"*. This will *always* be felt as *confusion* in the Believer's spirit with Evil *having agitated the indwelling Holy Spirit of God*.

> For God is *not* the author of *confusion*, but of peace, as in all churches of the saints. (1 Corinthians 14:33)

Paul ends this chapter on setting the *Biblical* "order" in the isolation of "*Speaking In Tongues*" and "*Praying In the Spirit*"[102] with this:

> Let all things be done decently and in order. (1 Corinthians 14:40)

Tracking:[103] What Is Salvation?™©[104]

The Holy Spirit possesses the spirit of Believers the moment of Salvation, this is the very definition of being "Born-Again". To be Born-Again is literally accepting Jesus as your God and Savior, and *it is the spirit of man that is Born-Again*[105] *by the new indwelling of the Holy Spirit.*[106] *The Believer is Born-Again as the consequence of the Holy Spirit instantaneously indwelling the spirit of the new Believer…* the very *definition of being "Saved"*.

If you are feeling contra-wise in your spirit about what is being peddled as "praying in tongues", this is a good sign in the Spirit that something is amiss.

Praying In the Spirit is a total release of the words coming out of the Believer's mouth… and giving total control to the Holy Spirit. *God's Language* is more Lifegiving and *Powerful* than anything that can

[102] For a Biblical differentiation between Speaking in Tongues and Praying In the Spirit see the upcoming chapter: 1 Corinthians Chapter 14: Made Simple.

[103] *Subject Tracking Boxes* are ™ and © by Third Awakening Foundation Inc.

[104] For a more in depth conversation on "Salvation" see: *Chapter 19. Appendix 4: To Know That You Know…*

[105] For How to Know You Are Saved see chapter: *Appendix 4: To Know That You Know…*

[106] John 3:1-8.

ever be spoken naturally by Believers.[107] When we *Pray in the Spirit*, the *Holy Spirit* literally *speaks* out to the Father, in His encoded *Language of GOD*! A Believer's *Prayer Language* cannot be understood by the Believer, nor anyone else, nor anything else.

Praying In the Spirit is for ***EVERY*** Believer:[108]

> Likewise the Spirit also helpeth our infirmities: for *we know not what we should pray* for as we ought [should]: but *the* [*Holy*] *Spirit itself maketh intercession for us with groanings [Rhema Words] which cannot be uttered* [except by GOD]. And he that searcheth the hearts [JESUS] knoweth what is the mind of the [Holy] Spirit, because he maketh *intercession* for [***all***] the saints according to the will of God [the Father]. (Romans 8:26-27)

Let's Set Some *Biblical* Parameters for "*Prayer Language*", and then We Will Flesh Them Out Using GOD's Word...

Decently and In Order:

There is no human "interpretation" of *Prayer Language*. It is a *Language of GOD*, by God the Holy Spirit, to God the Father on the Throne, under the *Authority* of the name of God the Son JESUS. This is GOD's preset order[109] defined by the GODhead[110] of the Three Personhoods of GOD in One GOD.

[107] For the word of God *is* quick, and powerful, and sharper than any twoedged sword, piercing even to the dividing asunder of soul and spirit, and of the joints and marrow, and *is* a discerner of the thoughts and intents of the heart. (Hebrews 4:12).

[108] Remember in contrast that Speaking In Tongues is only for a few Believers as chosen by GOD.

[109] Let all things be done decently and in order. (1 Corinthians 14:40).

[110] For the invisible things of him from the creation of the world are clearly seen, being understood by the things that are made, *even* his eternal power and **Godhead**; so that they are without excuse: (Romans 1:20).

Surrender Yourself and Your Time to GOD

Praying Always and *Praying Without Ceasing* is only possible by the Holy Spirit Who indwells all Believers' spirits. God the Father lives outside of time. Only the outworking of the indwelling Holy Spirit in Believers can accomplish keeping communication lines open to Heaven without break or pause. Yes, we pray through the Holy Spirit *even when Believers are asleep*!

When we apply ***GOD's Bible Puzzle Pieces Study Method*,**™[111] the meaning of any seeming *Biblical* inconsistency, becomes very *Simple* with absolutely no errors whatsoever. Go GOD!

Unbroken Prayers

[111] See especially the earlier chapter: *The Bible Puzzle Made Simple*.

And that is another spiritual mystery, to pray without ceasing, solved by using **God's *Bible Puzzle Pieces Study Method*™** of reconciling Scripture! There are *NO* contradictions in God's Word when properly discerned, when ***God's Bible Puzzle Study Method***™ is fully in place revealing God's final ***Perfect Bible Picture***™.

Prayer Language is absolutely *essential* in a Believer's *Spiritual Warfare* and as a background Prayer that is *always*, 24/7/365, keeps open communication with the Father on the Throne of God.

So let's suit-up and Fight the good Fight!

To paraphrase a well-known maxim:

Ask Not What God Can Do For You...

...Ask What You Can Do For God!

07. Ways to Let GOD Release Your Prayer Language:

Releasing the *Power* of the Holy Spirit
from Your spirit...

Back Up Against the Wall: My Personal Testimony...

This story is my personal testimony. I was battling for my life and desperate to hear from GOD. GOD seemed to me to be lost somewhere in the cosmos. I heard about a church that had "prayer rooms". I wasn't sure what that meant, but as I said, I was desperate. At that church I was called back into a designated "prayer room" and asked to stand up against a wall.

Now in my spirit this felt like a Holy Spirit driven encounter, but as a Baptist-boy I could have been up against a wall to be shot! (Funny, not funny). Since I was not offered a blindfold, I was fairly encouraged that there would be no flying lead today! This is where Faith steps in...[112]

As a legalistic "Baptist-boy" up against a wall, it wasn't as frightening as I expected, or having been misled to believe it would be. They

[112] For a much more in-depth discussion of Faith see author's Book: el Yerak, Dr Rhema; WALKING BY FAITH... What Is Faith, How To Live By Faith, and Finally Living the Victorious Christian Life!; Advanced Level Edition.

prayed over me with what I learned later was their "*Prayer Language*". They helped me, by "*jump starting*", in releasing my *Prayer Language*.

They began by speaking ***their*** "*Prayer Language*" *out-loud* and asked me to follow along to the best of my ability. Then they stopped praying in **their** *Prayer Language*, and told me to just continue by surrendering to the Holy Spirit and Pray in my own *Language*.

It worked! I felt the *Power* and *Presence* of the Holy Spirit arise on, and through me, like I had *never* felt before. The "Baptist-boy" in me had had my *Prayer Language* released! They literally helped me by taking my training wheels off! I left *Encouraged*, and I was feeling the Holy Spirit in a new, real, *Powerful*, in a tangible way!

Turn-Around[113]

I did not know the terms like "*Prayer Language*" and "*Praying In the Spirit*". I knew for certain that what I had experienced was approved before *GOD*, but again, the Baptist-boy in me *needed* as GOD directs, to verify this experience[114] in the *Bible*, *which conclusions you are reading here*. Again, for emphasis, we should *always* verify everything in GOD's Word. Upon verifying *Prayer Language* in the *Bible*, I discovered that it actually was *GOD's real and Amazing Prayer Language*! Go GOD!

I discovered that it was <u>*not*</u> the dreaded "*Tongues*" that I had been so sternly warned about so many times, but I had personally experienced the flow of GOD first-hand. *Finally... I had discovered what GOD said Praying In the Spirit really was!* By *wholly* trusting GOD,

[113] GOD told me that this year was my year of "turn-around".
[114] *All* things must be verified or denounced based *only* on GOD's *Holy Bible*.

I had surrendered years before to the Holy Spirit to *release* my *Prayer* Language*!* *It was, and is, a life-changing experience!* I wish that it had happened *years* before…

Praying In the Spirit made it so that I could actually *feel* the Holy Spirit swelling up inside of my spirit, and then flowing to the Throne of God in Heaven. It literally tethered me to God on His Throne in Heaven! I was literally *breathing* out the words of God, in God's Own Language! *WOW!*

But I knew that the experience and good feelings were *not* an empirical *Biblical verification*, so I went on a deep-dive in the Scriptures of the *Bible* using ***God's Bible Puzzle Study Method***™.

Praying In the Spirit creates a connection to the Throne of God like nothing that I had *ever* experienced, or even heard about. *Prayer Language radically transformed my life*, Christian ministry, and relationship with God!

Training Wheels:

I often use metaphors that might be familiar to most Readers. This helps some Believers to bridge the gap between head knowledge, and practical application. Sometimes, as in my case, the releasing of *Prayer Language* needs a bit of a "*jump start*". This is where an experienced Believer, one who has already learned how to *Pray in the Spirit*, helps jumpstart your *Prayer Language*, and you repeat what is coming out of their mouth. (Their *Prayer Language* is *not* your *Prayer Language*.)

A Helping Hand

This is like a parent teaching their child to ride a bicycle. The parent pushes the bike while balancing the child, then releases the beginner rider… To begin one's *Prayer Language*, this is where the experienced teacher starts, and then *"let's go"* and has the *Prayer Language* Trainee *"keep praying from their own heart"*[115]. This in taking off his proverbial training-wheels. As most parents can attest, *It works!…*

As in my personal experience in releasing my *Prayer Language*, this is often an excellent *"jump start"* to get one's *Prayer Language* started. *To help overcome stage-freight, and other hesitancies…*

Pop the Clutch: (Here Is One for the Men!)
I also liken beginning a Believer's Prayer Language. I liken it to starting a standard transmission car that the battery has given up. One person pushes the car to get momentum going, and then the person behind the wheel "pops the clutch", bypassing the powerless battery, and the motor roars to life! Let's get our Holy Spirit *Prayer Language* roaring to life Brothers and Sisters!

Let Loose Your Prayer Language… and Change the World!

Prayer Language puts *life* back into your relationship with GOD, and *Empowers* the Believer to do the "super-natural"[116] works of GOD. This is what GOD intended for all of us Believers to do all along[117]… Super-natural *Acts* of GOD through Believers are virtually impossible

[115] Praying always with all prayer and supplication in the Spirit, and watching thereunto with all perseverance and supplication for all saints; (Ephesians 6:18).
[116] Super-natural is defined as "above" the physical world and into GOD's spiritual realm. This phrase can be misused by the world where it usually refers to a non-GOD event, thereby corrupting the phrase. The "super-natural" as used here is in relation to the one True God JEHOVAH of the *Bible*. See also: JESUS and JEHOVAH or *Yeshua and Yahweh; What Difference Does It Make What We Call GOD and His Son Anyway? Advanced Level Edition.*
[117] Jesus said, And these signs shall follow them that believe; In my name shall they cast out devils; they shall speak with new tongues; They shall take up serpents; and if they drink any deadly thing, it shall not hurt them; they shall lay hands on the sick, and they shall recover. (Mark 16:18)

to accomplish without the release of GOD's *Power* by the Believer's *Prayer Language*.

Unconditional Surrender!

Don't Overthink It:

We men, have a tendency to overthink things. This is especially true of Believers with a Type-A personality. It effects men more than women. Remember *Prayer Language does not work by overthinking it. Natural thinking injects human thoughts and reasoning*. This is *NOT* to say we surrender our thoughts and prayers to any "spirit", but *ONLY* surrender to The Holy Spirit!

From the "Heart"...

In GOD's Word, the "heart" of the Believer usually refers to the core of the Believer's being where the soul joins the spirit of the Believer. The "heart" is the core of the person's decision making, memories, and emotions. This connection is also referred to as the "thoughts and intents of the heart"[118].

I *Pray in the Spirit* allowing my Prayers to be poured out from my heart as *Empowered* by the Holy Spirit. This silences outside

118 For the *word of God* is quick, and powerful, and sharper than any twoedged sword, piercing even to ***the dividing asunder of soul and spirit***, and of the joints and marrow, and is *a discerner of the thoughts and intents of the* ***heart***. (Hebrews 4:12).

interference, confusion, and static. This also helps focus on what the Holy Spirit is doing, rather than what you would be doing naturally.

Prayer Language is *Private, Unique* to each Believer, and *Not to Be Publicly Broadcast*:
I *Pray In the Spirit* quietly enough so that I myself cannot distinguish the words that are coming out of my mouth. This helps me eliminate interfering with God's Language. This can be especially helpful for beginners. Remember, *contrary* to those yelling in church, God's not deaf and you are not speaking to people, you are *Praying to God*.

The Love of God
Empowered by the Holy Spirit

Prayer Language is a *Private* Language from the Believer's heart, *Empowered* by the Holy Spirit, to the ears of the Father on the Throne.

> And when thou ***prayest***, thou shalt not be as the ***hypocrites*** are: for they love to pray standing in the synagogues and in the corners of the streets, ***that they may be se en of men***. Verily I say unto you, ***They have their reward***. (Matthew 6:5).

Quietly *Praying In the Spirit* can be helpful so as not to offend the person for whom you are Praying. This is especially helpful when you do not know if they are comfortable[119] with you *Praying In the Spirit*.

How Believers Can Receive Their Prayer Language:

- At the Moment of *Salvation.*
- By *Laying on of Hands.*
- By Hearing the *Rhema* Word *Spoken.*
- By *Praying* to Receive.

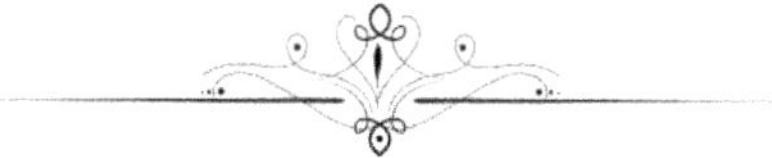

- At the Moment of Salvation:

> Who shall tell thee words, whereby thou and all thy house shall be *saved*. And *as I began to **speak** [Rhema* Words*], the Holy Ghost fell on them*, as on us at the beginning. (Acts 11:14-15)

- Laying On of Hands:

> Then *laid they their hands on them*, and *they received the Holy Ghost*. (Acts 8:17)

- Hearing the *Rhema* Word Spoken:

Every instance of *Praying In the Spirit* in the *Bible* was *out-loud*.

> While Peter yet *spake these words [Rhema* Words*]*, the Holy Ghost fell on all them which *heard the word* [*Spoken Rhema* Word]. And they of the circumcision which believed were astonished, as many as came with Peter, because that on the Gentiles also was poured out the gift of the Holy Ghost. For they heard them speak with tongues, and magnify God. Then answered Peter, Can any man forbid water, that these should not be baptized, which have received the Holy Ghost as well as we? (Acts 10:44-47)

- Praying to Receive:

[119] But take heed lest by any means this liberty of yours become a stumblingblock to them that are weak. (1 Corinthians 8:9).

> Who, when they were come down, prayed for them, *that they might receive the Holy Ghost*: (For as yet he was fallen upon none of them: only they were baptized in the name of the Lord Jesus.) Then *laid they their hands on them, and they received the Holy Ghost*. (Acts 8:15-17)

Non-Christians *CANNOT* Receive the Holy Spirit, therefore *Cannot* Receive *Prayer Language*:

> And when Simon [the sorcerer] saw that through *laying on of the apostles' hands the Holy Ghost was given*, *he offered them money*, Saying, *Give me also this power*, that on whomsoever I lay hands, he may receive the Holy Ghost. But Peter said unto him, *Thy money perish with thee, because thou hast thought that the gift of God may be purchased with money*. (Acts 8:18-20)

After being Saved, the most important Gift of the Spirit is *Prayer Language!*

Prayer Language enhances your relationship with God, *Empowers* Believers to do *Spiritual Warfare*, and *Edifies* the Believer.

If you can sense that there is more that God wants for you, releasing your Prayer Language most likely is the Key for a new successful Christian life, and a much more mature relationship with God.

We are only given a fixed amount of days on earth that are already numbered[120] by God. Make the most of your time you are given, because *time is precious* and cannot be recovered![121] God is focused on your finish line and all the things He needs to do throughout your

[120] So teach us to number our days, that we may apply our hearts unto wisdom. (Psalms 90:12).

[121] Seeing his days are determined, the number of his months are with thee, thou hast appointed his bounds that he cannot pass; (Job 14:5).

life to ensure you finish where He wants you to finish[122]. Again, Always Remember: ...Let Go, and Let God!

08. Everything Emanates from God's Agape Love:

Bible Study is not always Easy, but it is always Simple. God expects Believers to deep-drive and "study to show thyself approved unto God"[123]. You "courted" your spouse. Courting involves an *intentional* and targeted heart-to-heart relationship of "*chasing after your love*".

This means you naturally knew that you had to study their personality, find their likes and dislikes, whispering those sweet nothings, anticipate surprises, create intimacy, uplift them, and never belittle them in front of others.

You did not court your spouse, or future spouse, this way because you were "forced" to do so. You courted them from your heart, being driven and motivated by *Love*.

> As the hart [deer] panteth after the water brooks, so panteth my soul after thee, O God. (Psalms 42:1)

Being "forced" to do something for a spouse is *Hard*, acting from God's *Agape* Love makes it *Easy*. *Acts* of Love *Empower* Believers with

[122] But none of these things move me, neither count I my life dear unto myself, so that I might finish my course with joy, and the ministry, which I have received of the Lord Jesus, to testify the gospel of the grace of God. (Acts 20:24). I have fought a good fight, I have finished my course, I have kept the faith: (2 Timothy 4:7).

[123] *Study to shew thyself approved unto God*, a workman that needeth not to be ashamed, rightly dividing the word of truth. (2 Timothy 2:15).

God's *Agape* Love,[124] to *Love* God and *Act* accordingly. Some reading this might be cut to the quick by the indwelling Holy Spirit to return to your first love[125].

God Gave Me a very *Simple* Foundation for Ministry:

- Love the Unlovable

  and
- Be a Friend to the Friendless

On first blush, this sounds like an Easy Calling. However, putting these callings into *action* is *very* challenging endeavor. A case in point, the "unloved" are unloved for a reason! However, few Christians approach the unlovable, or the friendless. Yet these are the important ones that God is able to reach in Salvation. They can clearly see their own need.

> A man that hath friends must shew himself friendly: and there is a friend that sticketh closer than a brother. (Proverbs 18:24)

Closer Than a Brother

[124] el Yerak, Dr Rhema; WALKING BY FAITH... What Is Faith, How To Live By Faith, and Finally Living the Victorious Christian Life!; Advanced Level Edition.

[125] In the words of Jesus: Nevertheless I have somewhat against thee, because thou hast left thy first love. (Revelation 2:4).

This 1970s song: *He Ain't Heavy... He's My Brother*[126] has a message. This song was popularized by Neil Diamond in 1970 at the apex of the Vietnam War. The song was about two brothers on the battlefield... It is a sad indictment of the Fallen human nature that the unseen voice in this song calls after a brother carrying his brother. Taking a bit of poetic license, we may also understand this ballad as this man talking to God, for encouragement to accomplish the *Act* at hand of God's *Philo* (Brotherly/Family Love) Love, and *Agape* love. That is the definition of *Walking, by Faith*![127] (*Or in this case Running by Faith!*)

Our Love for Mankind Should Parallel the Believer's Love for God.

> If a man say, *I love* [God's *Agape* Love] *God, and hateth his brother*, he is a liar: for he that loveth [God's *Agape* Love] not his brother whom he hath seen, *how can he love* [God's *Agape* Love] *God whom he hath not seen?* (1 John 4:20)

One brother was mortally wounded and the other brother threw him over his shoulder and *ran* through the battle lines to get his brother to safety. (A Forrest Gump moment... Run Forrest, Run! But I digress...) This is a clear *Picture* of Jesus rescuing the perishing, and caring for the dying, from behind enemy lines.

God Gives Us Believers Supernatural Power by God's Agape Love to do the Humanly Impossible.

And if our heart is right, we don't give a second thought, we just jump into action! Here's Neil Diamond:

> He ain't heavy, he's my brother
> If I'm laden at all
> I'm laden with sadness
> That everyone's heart
> Isn't filled with the gladness
> Of love for one another

---

[126] Written by Scott, Bobby and Russell, Bob; *He Ain't Heavy... He's My Brother?*; Originally recorded by Kelly Gordon in 1969; Neil Diamond in 1970; Capitol Records .

[127] el Yerak, Dr Rhema; WALKING BY FAITH... What Is Faith, How To Live By Faith, and Finally Living the Victorious Christian Life!; Advanced Level Edition.

When Believers *Act* from GOD's *Agape* Love and direction, *nothing is impossible!*

> But I'm strong
> Strong enough to carry him
> He ain't heavy, he's my brother

This is GOD's Encouragement to the Believer to always, and only, *Act* in *Agape* Love. So, if you are going through a rough spot...

> *I can do all things through Christ* which *strengtheneth* me [by the Power of the Holy Spirit]. (Philippians 4:13)
>
> Finally, my brethren, *be strong* in the Lord, and in the *power* of his might [Holy Spirit]. (Ephesians 6:10)

Remember it's not by our insufficient power, but the omnipotent *Power* of GOD through the *Holy Spirit*. The Holy Spirit is the sum total *Power* of the entire Universe... and so much more![128] The *Power* of GOD is the Holy Spirit working *through* Believers.

Get Your Priorities Aligned with GOD:

> *But seek ye first the kingdom of God,* and his righteousness; and *all these things shall be added unto you.* (Matthew 6:33)

Chase After GOD:

Did you ever wonder why some Believers are so much closer to GOD?

> O God, thou art my God; early will I seek thee: my soul thirsteth for thee, my flesh longeth for thee in a dry and thirsty land, where no water is; (Psalms 63:1)

In human terms, a Believer's "first love" was intended to be our spouse. (On the spiritual level, a Believer's *Super-Power*[129] is GOD

[128] See Dr. Rhema's upcoming Book: The Holy Spirit: What Does GOD Say?.

[129] See especially the author's upcoming Book: There's a Superhero in Every Man: What does GOD Say?.

through us Loving the unlovable!) If your marriage is coming apart, maybe it's time for you to reinstate your *Agape* Love relationship with your spouse. Like Jesus our Bridegroom, you cannot force your spouse into an *Agape* Love relationship. But if you put *Agape* Love out there for your spouse, they usually respond in-kind.[130]

Let Go and Let God!

[130] See author's upcoming Book: el Yerak, Dr Rhema; *The Godly Wife: What Does God Say?; Basic Level Edition.*

Book Notes

09. Hinderances To Releasing Your Prayer Language:

Don't Listen to the Voices...

Tongues *Unbiblically* Taught as Demonic...
In a small private Christian school, we were taught that any supernatural "feeling" was of Satan, and an open door for demon possession. Well...

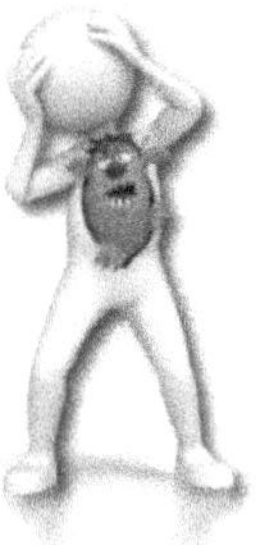

Christians *CANNOT* Be demon Possessed!

A *false "praying in tongues"* is, by its very nature, *of the Devil spirit*. It is a mocking *imitation* of God's *Language*. ***Only devils invert and distort the true Nature of God.*** With that said, just because Satan perverts God's Doctrines, is certainly *NO* reason to abandon God's true Doctrines. Otherwise God's work would be paralyzed because Satan *ALWAYS* *inverts* and *perverts* the Doctrines of God!

Christians *CANNOT* Be demon Possessed!:

> Ye *cannot* drink the cup of the Lord, and the cup of devils*: ye cannot be partakers of the Lord's table, and of the table of devils.* (1 Corinthians 10:21)
>
> We know that whosoever is born of God sinneth not; but he that is begotten of God keepeth himself, and *that wicked one toucheth him not.* (1 John 5:18)
>
> What? know ye not that *your body is the temple of the Holy Ghost which is in you*, which ye have of God, and ye are not your own? For ye are bought with a price: therefore *glorify God in your body, and in your spirit, which are God's.* (1 Corinthians 6:19-20)

As we can clearly see, there is no possible way that a Believer can "come under the control", be possessed, by a demon spirit during neither Prayer Language, Speaking in Tongues, nor at any time for that matter. *Demons can influence the Believer from the* ***outside***, called ***oppression***, *but demons* ***cannot*** *control the Believer from* ***within***, called ***possession***.

Satan ALWAYS Inverts and Perverts GOD's Word!

The Pride Trap:

Prayer Language ***is always*** *spoken out-loud* ***which releases GOD's*** *Rhema* ***Word*** *Power*. One of the ***traps*** of *Praying In the Spirit*, is ***pride***. The *Bible* equates "*pride*" with "*self-righteousness*". This is the *fake* and *evil* "*praying in tongues*".

When Believers want to be heard more than they want to really *Pray in the Spirit*, it comes from *hypocritical and self-promoting pride*.

Jesus addresses this self-aggrandizing of pride:

> And when thou prayest, ***thou shalt not be as the hypocrites are***: for they love to pray standing in the synagogues and in the corners of the streets, that they may be seen of men. Verily I say unto you, ***They have their reward***. But thou, when thou prayest, enter into thy closet, and when thou hast shut thy door, ***pray to thy Father which is in secret***; ***and thy Father which seeth in secret shall reward thee openly***. (Matthew 6:5-6)

Your worldly praises are your empty reward... They vanish like a mist:

> Whereas ye know not what shall be on the morrow. For what is your life? *It is even a vapour, that appeareth for a little time, and then vanisheth away*. (James 4:14).

Praying In the Spirit is ***not*** about your *self-righteousness*, but all about ***God's Righteousness***. It's about giving God the Glory and not trying to steal God's Glory for yourself. A Believer's *self-righteousness* will be its only reward in the praise of men now, but nothing in your hypocracy before God in eternity.

Too Self-Conscious:

Again, I want to emphasize here that Stage Fright can play a major role in releasing a Believer's *Prayer Language*. Believers must Act in the boldness[131] of God. Stage Freight is the opposite of Godly Faith.

Let the Holy Spirit Loose!

[131] And when they had prayed, the place was shaken where they were assembled together; and they were all filled with the Holy Ghost, and they spake the word of God with *boldness*. (Acts 4:31).

In Review:

Stage Fright:
It can be difficult for some people to let go of their conscious control of Prayer, and let the Holy Spirit have Control. It is the Holy Spirit that makes "*intercession*" for the Saints to the Throne of God[132] with *God's Prayer Language*.

The Christian *Men*'s *Stage-Fright* Dilemma:
Most men have a more difficult time being vulnerable, much more so than most women. Men are naturally more logical and much less emotional. It's the way God designed the genders. The outworking of the Holy Spirit is founded in *Surrender*. Men are made by God to be "in control". Men are therefore more susceptible to "*pride*" as mentioned above.

It's not about you... It's all about God!

Surrender...

In my experience with *Prayer Language*, *Stage-Fright* does affect men more than women. I have been blessed in being able to help hundreds of Christians allow God to release their *Prayer Language*.

[132] Likewise the [Holy] Spirit also helpeth our infirmities: for we know not what we should pray for as we ought: but the [Holy] Spirit itself maketh intercession for us with groanings which cannot be uttered [by Christians]. And he that searcheth the hearts knoweth what is the mind of the [Holy] Spirit, because he maketh intercession for the saints according to the will of God. (Romans 8:26-27).

Men were created by God for physical and *Spiritual Warfare* to fight Evil. Sometimes you have to put feet to your Faith. Men must exercise *humbleness* and *trust* in God to accommodate the *Spiritual*, that is the Holy *Spirit Empowered*, expression of *Praying In the Spirit*.

There is an inherent *vulnerability* in *Prayer Language*. This built-in *vulnerability* makes men *more anxious of failing and being humiliated in front of other people*. For this reason, men respond better in, as in my experience, to a *one-on-one* (with a silent standby) situation. Women can also struggle with "*stage-fright*" in its various forms.

Break-Out and Break-Through:

Humbleness is the Key to *Knowing* and *Growing* in the *Word of God*: You must be willing to let the Holy Spirit show you that you don't always know everything, even the things that you think you might already know. Unfortunately, many times *denominationalism* does not teach the pure Word of God. (Yes, I've seen the manuals) We owe our allegiance to God's Word, and certainty not the *commandments-of-men*.

Some *denominations* have taught incorrect *doctrine*, going unchallenged for so long in their denomination, that everyone just assumes it must be true. This is what the *Bible* calls the "*traditions-of-men*" and "*doctrines-of-devils*", which God says always conflicts with the actual "*Commandments of God*":

> Hearken, my beloved brethren, Hath not God chosen the poor of this world rich in faith, and heirs of the kingdom which he hath promised to them that love him? (James 2:5)

Humbleness and *Freedom* In *Surrender*

There is a reason that *Pride*, *Rebellion*, and *Stubbornness* are *Witchcraft* and *an anathema*[133] before God:

> For rebellion is as *the sin of witchcraft*, and *stubbornness* is as *iniquity* and *idolatry*. (1 Samuel 15:23)

All of the Aforementioned Can be Found in the Sin of Pride:

> *Pride goeth before destruction*, **and** *an haughty spirit before a fall*. (Proverbs 16:18)

Understanding

Not Having a *Biblical* Understanding:
As was mentioned earlier, ***God's Bible Puzzle Study Method***™ helps to insure we are "rightly dividing the word of truth".

Study, Study, STUDY...

[133] Cursed, or damned before God.

To Study God's Word and *"rightly dividing the word of truth"* is the Foundation of ***God's Perfect Bible Jigsaw Puzzle Piece Study Method***™.

> ***Study*** *to shew thyself approved unto God*, a workman that needeth not to be ashamed, ***rightly dividing*** *the word of truth*. (2 Timothy 2:15)

Sometimes Seeing the *Puzzle* for the *Pieces* Draws Our Eyes Away from the Total, "Big Picture":

The *Puzzle* Piece Is *Not* the Whole *Picture*

Unlearned:

"Unlearned" Christians are in danger of "self-destruction" when they live out the Christian life without first "learning" the required Scriptural Underpinnings on all given Doctrines or issue:

> As also in all his epistles, speaking in them of these things; in which are some things hard to be understood, which they that are *unlearned and unstable wrest* [wrestle], *as they do also the other scriptures*, ***unto their own destruction***. (2 Peter 3:16)

There are many Inhibiters to the releasing a Believer's *Prayer Language*. By going to God's Word, we can *overcome Inhibitions* which usually emanate from some form of *Pride* or *Fear*. The flesh is always at odds with the indwelling Holy Spirit, indwelling the spirit of the Believer.[134]

[134] For the flesh lusteth against the Spirit, and the Spirit against the flesh: and these are contrary the one to the other: so that ye cannot do the things that ye would. (Galatians 5:17).

Get out of the Driver's Seat and Make God your Engineer!

Trying to Engineer our own train is a formula for a *train wreck*! Move out of the way and let God take control!

The Main Takeaway to Inhibitions of *Prayer Language* is:

***...Let Go, and Let God*!**

...the End.

10. Practical Application: Practice, PRACTICE, PRACTICE!

Practice, Practice, PRACTICE…

To let God fully perfect your *Prayer Language* requires *Practice*. The outpouring of *Prayer Language* runs *contrary* to learned *natural human language*, as well as the *Fallen human nature*. *Natural language emanates from the Believers mind* and requires a conscious effort to speak and deliver the message that we intend. In contrast, *Prayer Language* is imparted from the Believer's *spiritual heart*. The responsibility for relaying our *natural language* is on the *natural man*,[135] the onus for *Prayer Language* is on God.

Natural language is in the *natural* realm, while God's *Prayer Language* is in the *spiritual* realm. We have practiced our natural language for years, and we must "***unlearn***" *the habits of natural language* to allow the Holy Spirit to create and transmit His *Prayer Language*.

Often it is difficult for Believers to let go of self-control and give that

[135] Of course God should always be intricately involved in all walks of our life.

control *up* to God. Remember this is a new experience for most Believers. Christians new to the exercise[136] of their *Prayer Language,* often need to overcome their *hesitancy* from years of being told *Prayer Language... does not exist*. Also being preached at from the pulpit that somehow *Prayer Language* is not of God. Again, *always* search[137] *God's Word* for ***"What Does God Say?"***, and do *not* rely on others to tell what they arrogantly think that God *should* have said.

Starting Over

Overcoming Bad Theology:

As we have previously explored, there are many bad ***"Biblical"*** *theologies* floating around out there. *Some bad theologies* arise from ignorance, and *some from premeditated Evil intent*[138]. Either way, the Believer suffers from an absence of their God-given *Prayer Language*.

This *bad theology* against *Prayer Language*, in particular, diminishes the Believer's effectual *Prayer*[139] life with God. It also greatly hampers the Believer's effectual *Power* in *Spiritual Warfare*[140].*You simply cannot fight Spiritual Warfare with the Armor of God without* the *most important* component of all... *Praying In the Spirit*:

[136] But refuse profane and old wives' fables, and exercise thyself rather unto godliness. For bodily exercise profiteth little: but godliness is profitable unto all things, having promise of the life that now is, and of that which is to come. This is a faithful saying and worthy of all acceptation. (1 Timothy 4:7-9).

[137] Search the scriptures; for in them ye think ye have eternal life: and they are they which testify of me. (John 5:39).

[138] See: Appendix 2. The devils Doing the Devil's Work...; subchapter: "Westcott & Hort Only" Controversy...

[139] ...The effectual fervent prayer of a righteous man availeth much. (James 5:16).

[140] See the conversation on Spiritual Warfare in chapter: *Ephesians Chapter 6: Spiritual Warfare*.

> *Praying always* with all prayer and supplication *in the Spirit*, and watching thereunto with all perseverance and supplication for ***all*** saints; (Ephesians 6:18).

Too many skip over verses 17-18 in the context of the *Armor of GOD*:
Too many skip over verses 17-18 in the context of the Armor of GOD, as if it were not part of the *Armor of GOD* at all. Not only is it part of the *Armor of GOD*, but ***Prayer Language*** is the ***Power*** **of GOD** that ***Empowers*** **the Believer** for ***Spiritual Warfare***.

The Apostle Paul goes on to emphasize the absolute necessity of *Praying In the Spirit*:

> And for me, that *utterance* may be given unto me, that I may open my mouth *boldly*, to make known the mystery of the gospel, (Ephesians 6:19).

Paul defines the word used here in Ephesians 6:19 as "*utterance*", elsewhere in Romans as "*Praying In the Spirit*":

> Likewise the *Spirit* also helpeth our infirmities: for we know not what we should pray for as we ought: but *the [Holy] Spirit itself maketh intercession for us* with groanings which cannot be *uttered* [by men]. (Romans 8:26).

Praying In the Spirit is ***Commanded*** by GOD for Believers!
Yes, you read that correctly... A Believer's *Prayer Language* is not only **necessary**, but *the Believer's use of Prayer Language is* ***Commanded*** *by GOD TO* ***ALL*** *Believers!* This Doctrine of GOD cannot be overemphasized.[141]

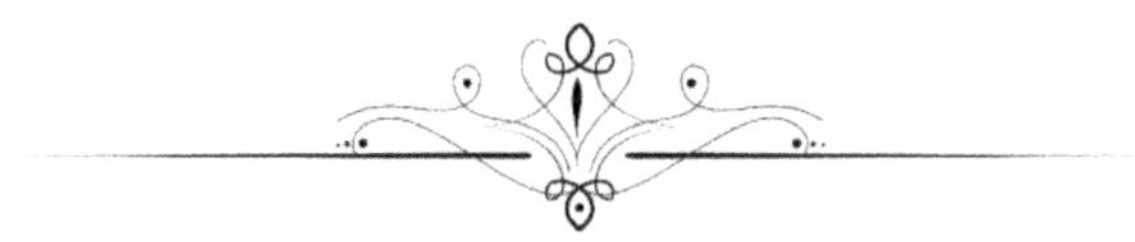

[141] See especially upcoming chapter: Believers are Commanded to Use Prayer Language!.

Surrender To God

Jesus profoundly condemned the "*traditions-of-men*". *Theology* is equivalent to *Bible* Critics bending and mauling God's Word.

> Howbeit ***in vain*** do they worship me, ***teaching for doctrines the commandments of men***. For laying aside the commandment [*Doctrine*] of God, ye hold the ***tradition of men***, as the washing of pots and cups: and many other such like things ye do. (Mark 7:7-8)

The *doctrines-of-men* are the "*doctrines of devils*":

> Now the [Holy] Spirit speaketh expressly [emphatically], that in the latter times some shall *depart from the faith*, *giving heed to seducing spirits*, *and doctrines of devils*; (1 Timothy 4:1)

As Born-Again Believers[142], Discipleship is essential in living the Victorious Christian life, and growing in our relationship with God. The *Bible* tells us we must quickly learn the milk of the *Basics* of the Faith, the *Basic* fundamentals of Salvation[143], then move on to the

142 Are you positively sure that you're a Born-Again Christian? For your answer to this question see chapter: *Appendix 4: To Know That You Know...*

143 Therefore *leaving the principles of the doctrine of Christ*, let us *go on unto perfection*; not laying again the foundation of repentance from dead works, and of faith toward God, Of the doctrine of *baptisms*, and of *laying on of hands*, and of *resurrection of the dead*, and of *eternal judgment*. (Hebrews 6:1-2).

meat of the Word of God. *This Book imparts the meat of the Scriptures…*

For the Believer with a *Whirling Mind*:
Prayer Language, as God intended, can overcome a "*whirling*" mind. Some of us cannot stop our minds from constantly thinking. (Type-A personality) This makes the "be still and know"[144] very difficult, and often impossible, to practice overcoming a "*whirling*" mind and spirit of men. *Prayer Language* circumvents a ceaseless mind. Remember that *Praying In the Spirit* *by-passes* the natural mind, like the "jump start" bypasses a dead car battery.

Practice, Practice, PRACTICE… literally, Practice makes Perfect!

The *Practice, Practice, PRACTICE* is the Believer "*Practicing*" in giving up wholly to God and His *Prayer Language*. *Practice, Practice, PRACTICE* is an *intentional* Action to align yourself with God.

The hardest part for the Believer is *staying out of God's way…* If you have a conscious thought about the words or sounds coming out of your mouth, then *it's of you*, and it is *not* *Praying In the Holy Spirit*. *Practice* makes *Perfect…*

Again, Always… Let Go, and Let God!

[144] *Be still, and know that I am God*: I will be exalted among the heathen, I will be exalted in the earth. (Psalms 46:10).

Book Notes

11. Prayer Language the Power of Spiritual Warfare!

Ready or Not, *Here Come the devils!*

The Power of Spiritual Warfare™©[145]

Prayer Languages are the *Languages of GOD*. No human, angel, nor devil can understand, nor discern the words of GOD. The *Power* of the Holy Spirit is released by the *Spoken Rhema Word*. To create the Universe, GOD *simply "spoke"* the Word (the *Rhema* Word) *out-loud*… and *"it was so"*[146].

Prayer Language is for the individual Believer for: *Spiritual Warfare*, Edifying and Empowering the Believer for Battle, and seeking guidance to *speak* the *Power* of GOD into others' lives. The Spoken *Rhema* Word releases that *Power* of the Holy Spirit to *create*, *destroy*, and *release*! As the *Bible* tells us, "*Power* is in the tongue"[147].

Praying In the Spirit ***Releases*** the *Power* of GOD:
Praying In the Spirit Releases the Power of GOD as it was in Creation when GOD said "let there be" and "it was" released accordingly, and made to be so. ***This is the*** *pent up, latent Power of GOD expectant to be Released*, like a pregnant woman. *Prayer Language* is *Spiritual Warfare* so that the individual Believer can *Speak out-loud the Power*

[145] *Subject Tracking Boxes* are ™ and © by Third Awakening Foundation Inc.
[146] Genesis chapter 1; See also upcoming chapter: *Ephesians Chapter 6: Spiritual Warfare*.
[147] Death and life are in the power of the tongue: and they that love it shall eat the fruit thereof (Proverbs 18:21).

so that the *Devil and his minions cannot understand* what we are *Praying*. *Latent Spiritual Power*, like an unborn baby ***expectant to be released!*** *Push!*

Prayer Language ***Confounds*** the Believer's Enemies:
If we spoke a *discernable* prayer out-loud, then the *Devil, who is always listening*, would hear us and know exactly where our struggles are! Let's say you are having trouble with lust for a certain individual. If you were to cry out to GOD in a discernable language, then *the Devil and his devils are listening, waiting, and ready to pounce accordingly*! Sin has consequences... Communication with the Father through the Holy Spirit is *incomprehensible to the enemy. Satan never sleeps and is always listening...* *Get into the FIGHT!...* As the US Special Forces *Battle-Cry* is shouted... *Oorah!!!*

The War is *REAL*!
The invisible *Spiritual War* of Evil Against GOD is extensively documented in the author's Book: *The Left's War Against GOD*[148]. A reminder:

> For we *wrestle* [fight] not against flesh and blood, but against principalities, against powers, against the rulers of the darkness of this world, *against spiritual wickedness* in high places. (Ephesians 6:12)

Prayer Language is the Power of the Holy Spirit Empowering the Believer's Spiritual Warfare. A Believer's Spiritual Battles can only be Empowered, Released, and Won through using the Believer's Prayer Language. Let's scare the Hell out of the devils! The Believer's Battle Armor is from GOD and ***is useless without Prayer Language. Prayer Language Empowers*** GOD's Armor and literally holds all of the pieces of the Armor together. We should always remember that *the Armor is "of" GOD*. This is GOD's Armor that the Holy Spirit lends to the Believer for *Spiritual Warfare*, to *ensure Victory*!!! *Scream... Oorah!!!*

[148] El Yerak, Dr. Rhema; The Left's War Against GOD! and The Right's RULES FOR ANTI-RADICALS!: A Call To ACTION!; : Volume 01; Master Level Edition.

12. Believers Commanded by GOD to Use Prayer Language

A Command ™©[149]

Let's See What GOD's Word Says About *Commanding* Believers to Use their *Prayer Language…*

Using *Prayer Language* is *Commanded*[150] by GOD to Believers:
Notice that *Praying In the Spirit* is a *Commandment of GOD* to *all Believers* to do *always*! The following verse is the parting reinforcement by the Apostle Paul of 1 Corinthians Chapter 14 telling us that *Prayer Language is Commanded by GOD* to Believers:

> If any man think himself to be a prophet, or spiritual, let him acknowledge that the things that I write unto you are the…… ………………*commandments of the Lord.* (1 Corinthians 14:37)

Believers are *Forcefully Commanded* by GOD to *Pray Always* and Without Ceasing[151]:
Did you catch the "*Commanded*" part? *Praying always* is only accomplished by yielding yourself to the indwelling Holy Spirit, Who continuously keeps the line of communication open to GOD on the Throne in Heaven.

> *Praying always* [a *Command*] with all prayer and supplication *in the* [*Holy*] *Spirit*, and watching thereunto with all perseverance and supplication for *all saints*; (Ephesians 6:18)

Pray Without Ceasing…

---

[149] *Subject Tracking Boxes* are ™ and © by Third Awakening Foundation Inc.
[150] (Please excuse the "slightly" *excessive* emphasis of this *Command* of GOD.)
[151] See especially the chapter: Believers Commanded by GOD to Use their Prayer Language!

This "*Praying*" in the above verse was *not* a newly created "tongue", not a new language of man, but the ability to speak the *Language of GOD* by the *Holy Spirit through the conduit of the Believer*. We should *never* forget that it is all about GOD, and not about us:

> For I say... to *every man* that is among you, *not to think of himself more highly than he ought* to think; (Romans 12:3)

The *Commandments* From GOD...

Believers Are Also *Commanded* to Use Prayer Language:

> *Praying always* [a *Command*] with all prayer and supplication *in the* [Holy] *Spirit*, and watching thereunto with all perseverance and supplication for *all* saints; (Ephesians 6:18)
>
> *Continue* [a *Command*] *in prayer*, and watch in the same with thanksgiving; (Colossians 4:2)

What too often happens, as with all "*traditions-of-men*", is a meaning is fashioned from the sinful and biased *imaginations of men*, who blasphemingly cherry-pick GOD's Word. They then regurgitate it up as though it is somehow "*Gospel*". Of course, the *Simplicity* and clear meaning only makes Sense and comes alive when using ***GOD's Perfect Bible Puzzle Pieces* Study *Method***™.

GOD Separates "*Speaking in Tongues*" from "*Prayer Language*":

> For he that *speaketh* in an unknown tongue [*Prayer Language*] *speaketh not unto men*, but *unto God*: for *no man*

> *understandeth him*; howbeit in the spirit he *speaketh* [*Prayer Language*] *mysteries*. (1 Corinthians 14:2)

GOD Commands Believers to use their Prayer Language for the Believer's edification, to receive special words for others, to *Empower* for *Spiritual Warfare*, and hold together and *Empower the Believer's Armor of GOD*.

*Prayer Language is the most **Powerful Weapon** of the Believer's Spiritual Arsenal*.

Everything Paul exhorts to Believers in this chapter is a *Command* of GOD for the Believer to *Act* upon, "*the things that I write unto you are the commandments of the Lord*"[152].[153]

From the Lips of the Believer…

The first time that *Speaking In Tongues* was spoken was at the releasing of the New Testament. Remember the Holy Spirit was *not* given to indwell Believers' spirits, until the moment of the First Day of Pentecost releasing the New Testament Era.

The New Testament Era is Literally Delineated by the Giving of the Holy Spirit to Indwell Believers.

Men and Angels Have Languages, which Should *Not* Be Confused With a Believer's *unique*, GOD-given *Prayer Language*:

There are earthly languages of men, and Heavenly Languages of angels. The "tongues" referred to in the above verse, the *tongues of both of men and of angels*… is *plural* indicating a plural number of languages. GOD is infinitely beyond simple men and angels. It could be reasonably deduced in *Scripture* that GOD has a *unique Prayer Language* for *each* and *every* Believer!

---

[152] If any man think himself to be a prophet, or spiritual, let him acknowledge that the things that I write unto you are the *commandments* of the Lord. (1 Corinthians 14:37)

[153] For a wider discussion of Paul's *commandments* are from GOD see chapter: *1 Corinthians Chapter 14 Made Simple*.

God Has Time In His Hands[154]

Paul Leads by Example:

> Wherefore also *we pray always* for you, that our God would count you worthy of this calling, and *fulfil all the good pleasure of his goodness*, and the work of faith with *power*: (2 Thessalonians 1:11)

How is it possible then, to pray nonstop 24/7? At first reading, this seems impossible, it may even seem a bit absurd. The *atheistic-mythologists* commonly dismiss nonstop prayer as a metaphor. For example, How can a Believer pray while they are asleep? *Pray Without Ceasing*: (Is That Even Possible?) But everything aligns into a ***Perfect Picture***™ when applying ***God's Bible Jigsaw Puzzle Pieces Study Method***™.

> *Pray without ceasing*. (1 Thessalonians 5:17)

This *Command* of God to Believers is to "*pray without ceasing*", has befuddled many Believers and is then summarily written off with some vague, contrived, or unGodly "*tradition of men*". First, we must identify this verse as a *Command* of God to Believers. But when we *Study* God's Word using ***God's Bible Jigsaw Puzzle Pieces Study Method***™, God's *Command* to Believers' to *Always Pray In the Spirit* suddenly becomes wholly understandable and functionally obvious. Let's now look at Ephesians 6 and God's ceaseless *Praying*.

154 God Has *ALL* Time in His Hands.

13. *Ephesians Chapter 6: Spiritual Warfare:*

Christians Are In a *Spiritual War...*
...Whether They Know It or Not!

This quote from a previous Book encapsulates this *Bible* Command.

> The greatest trick the Devil ever pulled,
> was convincing the world... he doesn't exist.[155]

Let's Dig In...

> Finally, my brethren, ***be strong in the Lord, and in the power of his might. Put on the whole armour of God***, that *ye may be able to stand against the wiles of the devil*. For we wrestle [fight] not against flesh and blood, but against principalities, against powers, against the rulers of the darkness of this world, against spiritual wickedness in high places. Wherefore take unto you the whole armour of God, that ye may be able to withstand in the evil day, and *having done all*, ***to stand. Stand*** therefore, having your loins girt about with truth, and having on the breastplate of righteousness; And your feet shod with the preparation of the gospel of peace; Above all, taking the shield of faith, wherewith ye shall be able to

[155] el Yerak, Dr. Rhema; JESUS and JEHOVAH or Yeshua and Yahweh; What Difference Does It Make What We Call GOD and His Son Anyway? Advanced Level Edition; chapter: The devils Who Did the Devil's Work...

> quench all the fiery darts of the wicked. And take the helmet of salvation, and ***the sword of the Spirit,*** *which is the* ***[Rhema]*** *word of God*: ***Praying always*** *with all prayer and supplication* ***in the Spirit***, and watching thereunto with all perseverance and supplication for *all* saints; (Ephesians 6:13-18)

First of all, notice that all the pieces of the Armor of God are for *ALL* the Saints. Paul concludes the Armor of God passage identifying that he is addressing "***all*** *the Saints*" [156].

> Finally, my brethren, be *strong* in the Lord, and in the *power* [Holy Spirit] of his *might*. (Ephesians 6:10)

This is a significant point in discerning between the "Gift of Tongues" and "*Prayer Language*", that they in fact are *not* the same. As throughly discussed, the "Gift of Tongues" is *only* for a *select few Believers for a specific time, and a specific situation,* as willed by the Holy Spirit[157]. Contrawise, "*Prayer Language*" is for *ALL* the.[158]

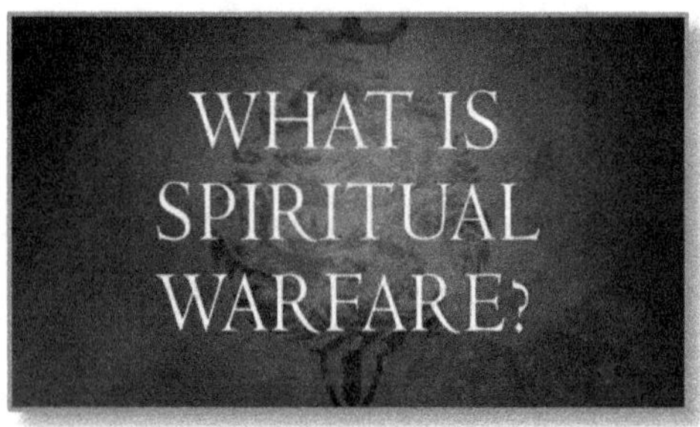

If You Don't Know, You're Already Losing!

Ephesians Chapter 6 is targeted on Christian *Warfare*, the *Armor of God*, and the *Power* to make it all work through the *conduit* of the individual Christian! *Praying* aloud, *In the Spirit*, is the *glue* and *Power*

[156] Ephesians 6:18.

[157] 1 Corinthians 12:11.

[158] See upcoming Book by Rhema el Yerak; Spiritual Warfare and the Armor of God: What Does God Say?.

that *holds the Believer's Armor of God together* and *Empowers the Believer for Battle!*

Prayer Language Is the Believer's Greatest *Weapon*

The Spoken *Rhema* Word and the Sword of the Spirit:

> And take the helmet of salvation, and *the sword of the Spirit, which is the word* ***[Rhema Word]*** *of God* (Ephesians 6:17)

The word "word" here is from the *Kone Greek* as the Spoken *Rhema* Word which releases the Power *of the Holy Spirit*. (This has been emphasized several times in preceding chapters)

When Jesus ***Destroys*** the remnant of the Antichrist, Jesus *speaks* the *Rhema* Word of the Holy Spirit:

> And the remnant were *slain with the sword* of him [*Jesus*] that sat upon the horse, which *sword* proceeded out *of his mouth* [*spoken*]: and all the fowls were filled with their flesh. (Revelation 19:21)

The Armor of God is often illustrated on a flannelgraph board as a Sunday School lesson for children. The problem is that *the Greatest piece of the Armor of God, is the spoken Rhema word,* and is almost

ALWAYS neglected and/or *naïvely* ***ignored at the Believer's peril***. *Spiritual Warfare is NOT a children's game*!

The Sword of the Spirit is the Spoken *Power Rhema* Word

Notice the *Biblical* relevance between the *Rhema* Spoken "Word" and the "S***word***" that proceeds out of the mouth of Jesus the Christ, which *Destroys* Evil. The *Rhema* word is the most *Powerful* Weapon of *Spiritual Warfare*.

> Wherefore also we *pray always* for you, that our God would count you worthy of this calling, and fulfil all the good pleasure of his goodness, and the work of faith with *power*: (2 Thessalonians 1:11)

Prayer Language *Empowers* the Believer to War:
Prayer Language is the *Missing Power* of the *Armor of God*.[159] *Praying In the Spirit* is the glue and *POWER* of the Christian's Armor. Ephesians chapter 6 is on Christian Warfare, the Armor of God, and the *Power of the Holy Spirit* to make it all work seamlessly together and in the *Power of God*!

[159] See the author's upcoming Book: The Holy Spirit IS the New Testament: What Does God Say?.

> *Praying always* with all prayer and supplication *in the Spirit*, and watching thereunto with all perseverance and supplication for ***all*** saints; And for me, that utterance may be given unto me, that I may open my mouth boldly, to make known the mystery of the gospel (Ephesians 6:18-19)

Above, is the summation of ***God's Bible Perfect Jigsaw Puzzle Pieces Study Method***™. God clearly teaches Believers that if you desire a *Breakthrough* in your Christian Walk, and Relationship with God, you must petition God to release your *Prayer Language*.

God Created the Whole Universe Instantly by *Simply* *Speaking* the *Rhema* Word:

God *Spoke* ***the*** *Power of the Holy Spirit* by which all things were Created:

> And God *said*, Let there be light: and there was light. And God *said*, Let there be a firmament in the midst of the waters, and let it divide the waters from the waters... And God *said*, Let there be a firmament in the midst of the waters, and let it divide the waters from the waters... And God *said*, Let the waters under the heaven be gathered together unto one place, and let the dry land appear: *and it was so*... And God *said*, Let the earth bring forth grass, the herb yielding seed, and the fruit tree yielding fruit after his kind, whose seed is in itself, upon the earth: *and it was so*... And God *said*, Let the waters bring forth abundantly the moving creature that hath life, and fowl that may fly above the earth in the open firmament of heaven... And God *said*, Let the earth bring forth the living creature after his kind, cattle, and creeping thing, and beast of the earth after his kind: *and it was so*... And God *said*, Let us make man in our image, after our likeness: (Genesis 1:3, 6, 9, 11, 20, 24, 26)

Its past time for your *Breakthrough*! "Having done all to *stand*, *STAND* therefore", and join the *fight* that you were born to *Fight*!

Breakthrough!

As we circle back to the beginning…

Again …Let Go, and Let God!

14. 1 Corinthians Chapter 14: Made Simple:

Making the Difference Between "*Tongues*" and "*Prayer Language*"... Simple, and Simply Understood:

It All Fits Flawlessly Together!

In 1 Corinthians chapter 14, Paul *compares-and-contrasts* "*Tongues*" and "*Prayer Language*". GOD *Simplifies* these two *different* and *mutually exclusive Biblical* Doctrines. "Seemingly" irreconcilable passages in the *Bible* are *Simply* solved and become unmistakably Clear to the seeking[160] Believer. This will all become crystal clear as we use ***GOD's Bible Jigsaw Puzzle Study Method***™.

1 Corinthians chapter 14 is *Simple*, but *not without*...

1.) using ***GOD's Perfect Jigsaw Puzzle Study Method***™
2.) ***comparing spiritual-things-with-spiritual*** [161]
3.) ***Keeping it Simple***[162]

We will also *compare-and-contrast* these 2 different *Bible* Doctrines. "Study" can incorrectly "appear" a bit intimidating. This can be

[160] Ask, and it shall be given you; seek, and ye shall find; knock, and it shall be opened unto you: For every one that asketh receiveth; and *he that seeketh findeth*; and to him that knocketh it shall be opened. (Matthew 7:7-8).
[161] Which things also we speak, not in the words which man's wisdom teacheth, but which the Holy Ghost teacheth; comparing spiritual things with spiritual. (1 Corinthians 2:13).
[162] 2 Corinthians 11:3.

especially intimidating given the cacophony of screeching demons when exposed to the Light. Devils swarm God's *inerrant* Word in an attempt to black out the Light of Jesus.

These devils operate like locusts overwhelming and sowing *confusion* and *discord* among Believers. Again, many of the so-called "'*bible*' *theologians*" and "'*bible*' *critics*" are actually self-identified *Luciferians*[163].

ANYONE who Identifies themselves as a "Bible Critic"... Is NOT a Christian, but a Ravenous Wolf in Sheep's clothing.

Confusion is a *dangerous weapon* of Evil used spuriously against Believers.[164] Following along, and all the ***Puzzle Pieces***™ of these 2 Doctrines, fall flawlessly into God's preordained ***Perfect Bible Puzzle Box Picture***™. The ***Puzzle Pieces***™ assembled of "*Speaking in Tongues*" and "*Prayer Language*" makes absolute and *Simple* Sense.

Sorting It All Out...

As you Study, remember that part of the *confusion* around 1 Corinthians 14 is recognizing to *which* of the 2 Doctrine it applies. As you use ***God's Bible Jigsaw Puzzle Study Method***™ this *Bible* Chapter

163 For an important and extensive *Study* on Satan's infiltration of the Church see following: *Appendix 2. The devils Doing the Devil's Work....*

164 See "confusion" in previous chapter: *Confusion In the Church*.

opens up, and makes it *Simply* sensible. ***GOD's Bible Jigsaw Puzzle Pieces Study Method***™ will keep your Study in context with the surrounding passages, and the *Whole* of the *Bible*.

---

1 Corinthians Chapter 14 is a Contrast and Differentiation Between "Speaking In Tongues" and "Praying In the Spirit".

Apparently the Corinthians were also somewhat *confused* on the subject of Believers' "Speaking In Tongues", "Prayer Language" and the *unbiblical* "*praying in tongues*". As demonstrated, this errancy has caused a great deal of damage throughout the Church Age. What most *Bible* "*commentators*" miss is that 1 Corinthians chapter 14 is *NOT* about "Tongues", but about the *difference* between "*Speaking In Tongues*" and "*Praying In the Spirit*", and overarching *Prophesy*.

Too often these pretend "*theologians*" begin with a preconceived *bias* of *what they insist that GOD should have said*, and miss the blessings of GOD, for the "*doctrines of devils*". They follow their Heathen "gods" in lockstep on their march to Hell.

Too Many Theologians, Not Enough GOD!

The *Doctrines-of-Men* are actually *commandments-of-devils*:

But in *vain* they do worship me, *teaching for* [*substituting*

> GOD's] *doctrines* [*for*] *the commandments of men*. (Matthew 15:9)
>
> Now the [Holy] Spirit speaketh expressly [emphatically], that in the latter times some shall *depart from the faith*, *giving heed to seducing spirits*, *and doctrines of devils*; (1 Timothy 4:1)

1 Corinthians 14 has been one of the Devil's most effective weapons used to *confuse* and execute a *sustained attack on GOD's Word and His people*. But when we apply ***GOD's Bible Puzzle Pieces Study Method***™, the confusion quickly falls away. 1 Corinthians 2:14 in ***comparing-spiritual-things-with-spiritual***, the beauty and the *Simplicity* of this chapter then becomes *Easily* determined.

> Which things also we speak, not in the words which man's wisdom teacheth, but which the *Holy Ghost* teacheth; *comparing spiritual things with spiritual*. But the natural man receiveth not the things of the Spirit of God: for they are foolishness unto him: neither can he know them, because they are ***spiritually discerned***. (1 Corinthians 2:13-14)

In 1 Corinthians 14:2-18, Paul explains the *difference* between "*Speaking* in Tongues" and "*Praying* In the Spirit". If these two were one Doctrine, then this entire *Bible* chapter would be *schizophrenic* and *nonsensical*. This is what the Devil would have you believe. By *confusing* these Doctrines, Satan has been able to scare the Brethren away from **GOD's most *Powerful* Spiritual Weapon** against the Devil.

In other words, it would be *contradictory and confusing*! GOD is neither schizophrenic, nor confusing. These deceiving "*theologians*" twist Scripture and bend it to their *evil intent*. Remember that *only a Spirit filled Believer can discern Scripture.*[165] *As with all of Scripture,*

[165] Which things also we speak, not in the words which man's wisdom teacheth, but which the Holy Ghost teacheth; comparing spiritual things with spiritual. But the natural man

the solution is always Simple. These verses are broken up into two categories contrasting and comparing "Prayer Language" and Spirit filled Believer can discern Scripture, the solution is always *Simple*. These verses are broken up into two categories *contrasting and comparing "Speaking in Tongues"* and "*Prayer Language*", with the broader Gift of *Prophesy*:

The Breakdown by Verse of 1 Corinthians 14:

⇨ 1. Verses 2-4 are Paul defining *Prayer Language*.

⇨ 2. Verse 5 Paul Downplays *Speaking in Tongues*.

⇨ 3. Verses 6-13 Is the Uselessness of *Speaking in a Tongue* that No One can Understand.

⇨ 4. Verses 14-18 Paul exhorts that in a Church assembly; we can only Bless others in a language *Understandable to the Church*.

⇨ 5. Verses 19-25 tell us that Prophesying is infinitely more important to the Church than *Speaking in Tongues*.

⇨ 6. Verses 26-40 give guidelines on the orderly use, and give proper place to Prophesying and *Speaking in Tongues*.

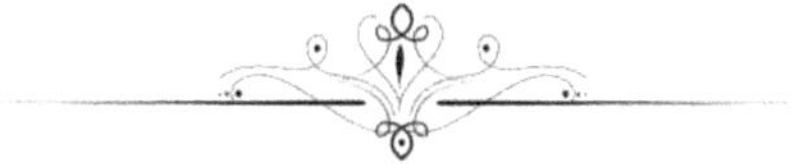

⇨ 1. Paul Defines *Prayer Language* (verses 2-4)

"*Prayer Language*" edifies only the individual Believer.[166] "*Speaking In Tongues*" is a commonly used human language that edifies the Believers who can hear and *understand*:

> For he that speaketh in an unknown tongue *speaketh* not unto men, but **unto God**: for *no man understandeth him*; howbeit *in the **spirit** he speaketh mysteries* [*uninterpretable Words of God*]. But he that prophesieth speaketh unto men to edification, and exhortation, and comfort. He that

receiveth not the things of the Spirit of God: for they are foolishness unto him: neither can he know them, because they are spiritually discerned. (1 Corinthians 2:13-14).

166 Jude 1:20.

speaketh in an unknown *tongue* edifieth himself; *but he that prophesieth edifieth the church*. (1 Corinthians 14:2-4)

⇨ 2. Paul Downplays Speaking in Tongues (verse 5)

Remember in 1 Corinthians 12:28 Paul documents "*Speaking in Tongues*" as the least of all the gifts of the Holy Spirit.

> I would that ye all spake with *tongues*, but rather that ye *prophesied*: *for greater is he that prophesieth than he that may receive edifying*. (1 Corinthians 14:5)

⇨ 3. The *Uselessness* of *Speaking in a* ***Tongue*** where No One can Understand (verses 6-13)

Believers ***must*** understand that "*Interpretation of Tongues*"[167] is in the foreign tongue/language being spoken to the unbeliever, or what use would it possibly be? When someone stands up in Church and blurts out a "*tongue*" someone else there *MUST* be able to "*Interpret*". Otherwise it's just someone who "*speak*[s] *into the air*":

> Now, brethren, if I come unto you *speaking with tongues, what shall I profit you*, except I shall speak to you either by [something that you can understand] revelation, or by knowledge, or by prophesying, or by doctrine? And even things without life giving sound, whether pipe or harp, except they give a distinction in the sounds, how shall it be known what is piped or harped? For if the trumpet give an uncertain sound, who shall prepare himself to the battle? So likewise ye, *except ye utter by the tongue* words easy to be understood, how shall it be known what is spoken? *for ye shall speak into the air*. There are, it may be, so many kinds of voices [languages] in the world, and none of them [the earthly languages] is without signification [understanding]. Therefore if I know not the meaning of the voice, I shall be unto him that speaketh a barbarian, and he that speaketh shall be a barbarian unto me. Even so ye, *forasmuch as ye are*

[167] See chapter: Gifts of Tongues & Interpretation of Tongues.

> *zealous of spiritual gifts, seek that ye may excel to the edifying of the church*. Wherefore let him that speaketh in an unknown tongue pray that he may *interpret*. (1 Corinthians 14:6-13)

⇨ 4. We can only Bless in a Language Understandable to Others. (verses 14-18)

"*Praying In the Spirit*" blesses us, but not others. We pray and sing in the Holy Spirit for our own edification and empowerment, and we *pray out-loud* in a language understood by others, to bless others. *How do others receive a blessing if they cannot understand what we are praying or singing*? No one can "understand" *Prayer Language*. As such, it only edifies the individual Believer who is "*Praying In the Spirit*".

> For if I *pray* in an unknown *tongue*, my spirit prayeth, but my understanding is unfruitful. What is it then? I will pray with the spirit [where only God understands], and I will pray with the understanding also [so others understand]: I will sing with the spirit [where only God understands], and I will sing with the understanding also [so others understand]. Else when thou shalt bless with the spirit, how shall he that occupieth the room of the unlearned say Amen at thy giving of thanks, seeing he understandeth not what thou sayest? For thou verily givest thanks well, but the other is not edified [who cannot understand]. I thank my God, I speak with *tongues* more than ye all: [because you are messing this *Tongues* thing up!] (1 Corinthians 14:14-18)

⇨ 5. Prophesying is Infinitely more Important to the Church than Speaking in Tongues. (verses 19-25)

> Yet in the church I had rather speak five words with my understanding, that by my voice I might teach others also, *than ten thousand words in an unknown tongue*. Brethren, be not children in understanding: howbeit in malice be ye children, but in understanding be men. In the law it is written, With men of other tongues and other lips will I speak unto

this people; and yet for all that will they not hear me, saith the Lord. *Wherefore tongues are for a sign, not to them that believe, but to them that believe not: but prophesying serveth not for them that believe not, but for them which believe.* ***If therefore the whole church be come together into one place, and all speak with*** *tongues,* ***and there come in those that are unlearned, or unbelievers, will they not say that ye are mad?*** *But if all prophesy, and there come in one that believeth not, or one unlearned, he is convinced of all, he is judged of all*: (1 Corinthians 14:19-25)

⇨ 6. Guidelines on the orderly use, and proper place, to "*Prophesy*" and "*Speak in Tongues*". (verses 26-40)

How is it then, brethren? when ye come together, every one of you hath a psalm, hath a doctrine, hath a tongue, hath a revelation, hath an *interpretation*. *Let all things be done unto edifying. If any man speak in an unknown tongue, let it be by two, or at the most by three, and that by course; and let one interpret.* But *if there be no interpreter, let him keep* ***silence*** *in the church* [***because it is Prayer Language not Tongues!***]; and let him *speak to himself, and to God*. Let the prophets speak two or three, and let the other judge. If any thing be revealed to another that sitteth by, *let the first hold his peace*. For ye may all *prophesy* one by one, that all may learn, and all may be comforted. And the spirits of the prophets are subject to the prophets. For *God is not the author of confusion, but of peace, as in all churches of the saints*. Let your *women keep silence in the churches*: for it is not permitted unto them to speak; but they are *commanded* to be under obedience, as also saith the law. And if they will learn any thing, let them ask their husbands at home: for *it is a shame for women to speak in the church*. What? came the word of God out from you? or came it unto you only? If any man think himself to be a prophet, or spiritual, let him acknowledge that *the things that I write unto you are the commandments of the Lord*. But

> if any man be ignorant, let him be ignorant. *Wherefore, brethren, covet to prophesy, and forbid not to speak with tongues. Let all things be done decently and in order.* (1 Corinthians 14:26-40)

Everything Paul exhorts in 1 Corinthians 14, is a *Command* of God to *all* Believers, *"the things that I write unto you are the commandments of the Lord"*! (verse 37) Many a Believer, theologian, pastor, and *Biblical* teacher has stumbled over this *Bible* chapter. *Evil tries to read-in the doctrines-of-men*, and *fail to actually read-out of the Scriptures*.

When 1 Corinthians 14 is read for what God is *actually* saying, it is *Simple*. This Chapter was intended to clarify the *differences between "Speaking In Tongues"* and *"Praying In the Spirit"*. We should always read the *Bible* with the eyes of a child[168] for the *Simplicity* that's only in Christ Jesus.

When we see 1 Corinthians Chapter 14 using ***God's Bible Jigsaw Puzzle Pieces Study Method***™, and overcome the cacophony of demonic voices, *Paul's meaning becomes crystal clear*.

1 Corinthians 14 sorts out all the confusion between *"Speaking In Tongues"* and *"Praying In the Spirit"* and the false *"praying in tongues"*. There is a clear difference between *"Speaking In Tongues"* and *"Praying In the Spirit"*. Always remember that God's Word is *Simple*, while men's perspectives are foolishly complex, damaging, and can even be damning. A correct understanding of God's Word is necessary to avoid damnation, and an error filled Christian Walk.

[168] And whoso shall receive one such little child in my name receiveth me. (Matthew 18:5).

Book Notes

15. Postscript: Be Blessed!

As we circle back to the beginning, I pray that your heart has been pricked, surrendered, and blessed! *Nothing good ever comes from nothing*. We have to do ***something*** in the name of GOD, to get something out of it.

I pray your *Journey* takes you far, and blesses you more in the Lord GOD.

This is Your New Beginning…

…Make the Most of It!

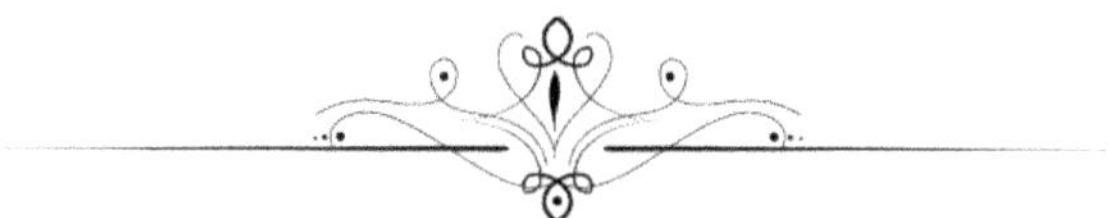

Book Notes

16. Appendix 1: The ShaNaNa Delusion:

The *Sha-Na-Na* Delusion

Prayer Language: It's *NOT* a Repetition of a Few Random Syllables! *Sha Na... Na, Na... Na, Na... Na, Na... Na...* chirps the *pretender*. There is a lot of pressure in some Christian circles to *force* a Believer to "*pray in tongues*", whether real, or *not*,[169] as "*proof*" of their Salvation. Of course, there is no such thing as "*praying in tongues*".

This leads many Christians to employ the *imaginary "Sha-Na-Na" Delusion*. This Delusion is *a demonic imitation* to actually "*Praying In the Spirit*". *Most Christians have never been properly taught what the Bible teaches us about Speaking In Tongues*, and *Praying In the Spirit*.

I have heard the *majority* of those who claim to be "*praying In tongues*" using this meaningless repetition of a few empty syllables, which is *almost always*... *Sha Na... Na, Na... Na, Na... Na, Na... Na, ad nauseum*. The end sounds like the cadence of an automatic weapon... Rat-a-tat-a-tat-a-tat-a-tat-tat-tat .... *Not good, Not God!*

[169] See: Appendix 3: Tongues Not a Required Confirmation of Salvation.

The near universality of this phrase implies that it is from the same Evil source. The only 2 options are God, and Satan. As we have unquestionably verified, it is *NOT* of God, *but it is of Satan*.
I have had the amazing God-ordained opportunity to take my ministry to *5 different Continents*, and verify the "*ungodly*" false *doctrine* of "*praying in tongues*", which is on all accounts, Universal. I have witnessed this false "*praying In tongues*" "*Sha-Na-Na*" *Delusion* on all *5 of these Continents.* The Devil has a network of devils *mimicking* and *mocking* the ministry of Jesus across the world.

A *real* language flows freely and has a vast resource of words. (The English language, for instance, has over a million words. You caught that right? Words, not syllables) A *true* language is not limited to a few repeated syllables Rat-a-tats. *How much more so then, do you think are the deepness and richness of the Languages of God*?

The "Sha, Na, Na" Demonic Imitation:

In practice it's more like... Sha...na, na... na, na...
na, na... na, na... ad nauseam

Prayer Language is *Not* Vain Repetition:
Jesus admonishes us:

> But when ye pray, ***use not vain repetitions**, **as the heathen do***: *for they think that they shall be heard for their **much speaking***. (Matthew 6:7)

Vain means "*meaningless*". *Prayer Language* is not a "magic" mantra, as the bookish command "*Open Sesame*" from the *One Thousand and One Nights* also known as, *Arabian Nights*[170]. You're not in control, God is, and *you cannot conjure-up God!*

---

[170] Burton, Sir Richard; New York; Charles Scribner's Sons; 1909.

It is also worth noting that JESUS is making a direct comparison between all "*heathen*" religions, and the *Christian Faith*. JESUS makes it clear that there are *only 2 religions in the* world, Satanic *Heathenism*, Paganism in all non-Christian religions in all its multitude of manifestations, and *Christ*ianity.[171]

Focus on GOD, and not what's coming out of your mouth. *Prayer Language is about Surrender, giving the Holy Spirit control of your words.* This is the *Rhema* Word of GOD *spoken* to *release the Power of God through the Holy Spirit*.

Sha, Na, Na is *not* "praying",
it's a passé singing group!

Sha, Na, Na... Blah... blah...blah
Prayer Language is *not* a mantra.[172] (Yes, the use of "mantra" is intentional as mantras are *Heathen* and demonic at their core.) *Prayer Language* is exactly that... *a Language*.

Prayer Language is *not* a series of vain, meaningless, and repeated syllables. This is what *Heathens*, who are *Luciferians*, do in ***nauseating*** repetition. A mantra is *not* Christian. A mantra is a repetitive *Heathen jargon used to summon devils*! We must be careful to always test the spirits and see if they are of GOD or Satan.

[171] He that is not with me is against me; and he that gathereth not with me scattereth abroad. (Matthew 12:30).

[172] *Webster's Dictionary*: A sacred verbal formula repeated in prayer, meditation, or incantation, such as an invocation of a god, a magic spell, or a syllable or portion of scripture containing mystical potentialities.

> Beloved, believe not every spirit, but *try the spirits whether they are of God*: because many false prophets are gone out into the world. (1 John 4:1)

So why then would Christians use devil worship mantras in summoning devils, as *Luciferian Heathenism* Who intentionally exploit God's *Prayer Language* ***into*** "*praying in tongues*"? (If you see no problem mixing God's Word with Pagan devil worship, you should skip directly to: *Appendix 4: To Know That You Know...*)

Prayer Language is not Heathen "magic" whereby the Holy Spirit is "summoned". The Holy Spirit already and continuously resides *within* the spirit of the Believer. The Holy Spirit's *edification for the Believer occurs from within*, *not from without as Heathen*, and Luciferian "*magic*"[173] *does*.

Stay away from the *Sha...na, na... na, na... na, na... na, na... Delusion*: The "modern" Christian Church has incorporated many Heathen practices, camouflaged under the false façade of Christianity. *This is a major factor of the* ***in****effectiveness in the "modern" Christian "religion" it's not Christian*!

Christianity has tragically adopted Heathen, Pagan, and Luciferian practices and beliefs which are *mockeries* of Christianity and the One, True God.

Let's get the mocking *sha-na-na* **out of our churches** *now-now-now!* *And follow* ***God's Bible Jigsaw Puzzle Pieces Study Method***™ to

...Get the Holy Spirit Back in our churches!

---

[173] For a deeper study on Luciferians "magic" see: el Yerak, Dr. Rhema; Jesus and Jehovah or Yeshua and Yahweh; What Difference Does It Make What We Call God and His Son Anyway? Advanced Level Edition; chapter: The devils Who Did the Devil's Work...

17. Appendix 2. The devils Doing the Devil's Work...[174]

It is *critical* for Christians to have at least a basic understanding of how the Devil has *"crept in unawares" infiltrating most Christian "churches"*. These Luciferians ***subtly*** *infect the minds* of a myriad of Christian Believers. We will look at the three most evil of the Devil's influencers: B. F. Westcott, F. J. A. Hort, and James Strong... *the Devil's trinity of Evil... The devils Who Did the Devil's Work...*

Brooke Westcott

Fenton Hort

James Strong

There is, and has been, a most dominant Confederacy of modern *"'bible'* critics", *"**re**-Translators"*[175] and ***re**-Versionists*. These have *secretly* woven Evil throughout the true *Bible in a 1,000+ counterfeits* in the form of 1,000+ ***re**-Versions.* They created over ***1,000+ Luciferian**, counterfeit "'bible' Versions"*. We will consider the three most dominant of these *"theologians"*, *self-identified "'Bible' critics"*, and *self-avowed Luciferians* who have done the most injury in turning God's Holy Word... into an ode to Satan.

These are the three devils that did the most ruinous work of the Devil

[174] There is a continuity device employed especially in these two chapters. Please have patience with the process. There are interconnected plays-on-words using highlighted terms such as: ***re**-Versions*, ***re**-Versionists*, ***re**-Translators*, *et al.* As you read it will become more evident of the use of these terms in *glow*.

[175] I have ***re**-Created* several words, a sort of ***re**-Purposing* birthed from other words to emphasize the lunacy of the *evil Confederacy*.

Against *GOD's Holy* Word. In case you do not see the magnitude, there are many *millions* of souls today *in Hell* because of this *evil Confederacy*! These devils still haunt the Church today...

It's time for an Exorcism Out of the Churches, and Off of Believers![176]

One should begin to smell the suffocating fumes of Sulphur rising up when someone announces their intention to "criticize" the Bible, the Holy Words of GOD!

Testimonies of the Devil...

In 1887, the founder of "*Lucifer*" *Magazine* Helena Petrovna Blavatsky (1831-1891), and editor Annie Besant (1847-1933), *along with other occultists* ***believed that*** ***Christian*** *churches were the key to introducing the doctrines of Lucifer to large masses of people*. The 1904 annual report of the *Theosophical Society* stated:[177]

> "I believe it is *through the* ***[Christian]*** *Churches* and not through the Theosophical Society that *Theosophy* [the worship of Lucifer]... *must and should come to large bodies of people in the West*."[178]

And then just eight years later the 1912 report of the *Theosophical Society* stated:

> Our [*Luciferian*] *Lodges* continue their *propaganda* work.... Outside the Lodges many of the members engage *in what is really Theosophical work* such as lecturing, talking on the principles we are trying to put forward, *preaching* and other

---

[176] See the author's upcoming book: el Yerak, Dr. Rhema; Curses and Christians: What Does GOD Say?.

[177] David J. Stewart; *Occult Roots of The Modern Bible Versions*; October 2014, and following.

[178] H. P. Blavatsky, Annie Besant; *Transactions of the Theosophical Society*; 1904, p. 377.

> activities *in connection with the Christian Churches* and other organizations....[179]

The nineteenth century occult mystic Fenton **Hort**, is perhaps best known for his part in the work of the corrupt "bible *Revision Committee*" *[**re-**Version]* of 1881. Speaking on the subject of creating a "*new*" eclectic [*One World religion*] New Testament text, Hort stated:

> At present very *many orthodox but rational men are being unawares*[180] acted upon by [devil] influences which will ...*acted upon by* [***devil***] *influences which will assuredly bear good fruit in due time*, if the process is allowed *to go on quietly*; [181]

And *quietly* it did...

I thought it prudent here to recall an additional three verses from God's Word showing how Satan uses evil men to *secretly corrupt* the *Holy and Pure Word of God* and "change", "transform", and "pervert" *God's True Word*, into a *Lie*...

> Who ***changed*** *the truth of God* ***into a lie****, and worshipped and served the creature* [the ***Devil***] *more than the Creator* [God], who is blessed for ever. Amen. (Romans 1:25)

There are Devil's disciples today parading as "Christians" in almost every "church". As the following passage tells us, the "church" has been *infiltrated at all levels including pastors and leadership*:

---

[179] Annie Besant; *Theosophist Magazine*; 1912, p. 88.

[180] Beloved, when I gave all diligence to write unto you of the common salvation, it was needful for me to write unto you, and exhort you that ye should earnestly contend for the faith which was once delivered unto the saints. For there are certain *men crept in unawares*, who were before of old ordained to this condemnation, *ungodly men*, turning the grace of our God into lasciviousness, and denying the only Lord God, and our Lord Jesus Christ. (Jude 1:3-4).

[181] Life and letters of Fenton John Anthony Hort, Vol. 1, 1896, p. 400.

> For such are ***false apostles***, ***deceitful workers***, *transforming themselves into the apostles of Christ*. And no marvel; for Satan himself is transformed into an angel of light. *Therefore it is no great thing if his* [*Satan's*] *ministers also be transformed as the ministers of righteousness*; whose end shall be according to their works. (2 Corinthians 11:13-15)

Per-Verting the Gospel is the work of *witchcraft*. For proper emphasis of *damnation* of being "*accursed*" is repeated here twice in only 2 verses:

> O foolish Galatians, who hath *bewitched* you, that ye should not obey the truth, before whose eyes Jesus Christ hath been evidently set forth, crucified among you? Which is not another; but *there be some that trouble you, and would pervert [**per**-Vert] the gospel of Christ.* But though we, or an angel from heaven, **preach any other gospel unto you than that which we have preached unto you**, *let him be **accursed***. As we said before, so say I now again, If any man preach any other gospel unto you than that ye have received, *let him be **accursed***. (Galatians 1:7-9)

...The devils Who Did the Devil's Work, continued...

As noted, three of the most *wicked of the devils Who Did the Devil's Work...* were **Westcott**, **Hort**, and **Strong**. I have read *hundreds* of books, dissertations, theses, and papers about each of these men, this ungodly *triad of Lucifer*. However, I will distill these thousands of pages down into a few well-informed pages...

Hold on and I guarantee you will be Blessed by the way this chapter ends!

Westcott & Hort

The *Received Text, King James Bible* (*KJB*) testifies *against **All*** other "modern" English "bible" translations, ***re-****Versions,* ***re-****Translations*, and ***re-re****-Translations parading* as the genuine "*Holy Bible*". Just because a "*Version*" has "Holy *Bible*" stamped on its cover, does *not* mean that it is in fact "Holy", nor a real "*Bible*".

Of the over 1,000+ English "'*bible' Versions", there can ONLY be One True Word of God*... The *Received Text Bible* (*KJB*). ***All*** other of the remaining 1,000+ "*Versions*" *[**re-**Versions, **per**-Versions]* are derived from the *Luciferian Westcott & Hort corrupted "**new**" Greek New Testament [**pre**-Versions and **re-re**-Translations]*.

The resultant "*translations*", are not really "*translations*" at all, but are *intentionally [**pre-**Purposely] corrupted* into "***re-re-****Translations",* "***re-****Versions*", "***re-****Interpretations*", *et al*, are from **con**-*Verts* of men [**con**-*Men*] ***attempting to put man's words... in God's mouth***! *God Forbid!*[182]

I am absolutely persuaded[183] that God does not take kindly to this abomination, nor to the Abominators. All these alternate corrupted "reinterpretations" and ***re-****Versions* have their root in the *Westcott & Hort Only* "***scheme***" to corrupt **God's Perfect *Bible***!

And Corrupt They Did...

The devils Hiding behind Luciferian "'*bible' Versions*'" *[**re-Versions**]*: The word "*Version*" concerning the 1,000+ corrupted "*Versions*" *[**re-**Versions]*, is as the Luciferians labeled this "*scheme*" as a *propaganda* device. The Luciferian ***re****-Translators schemed* to label

---

[182] What shall we say then? Is there unrighteousness with God? God forbid. (Romans 9:14).
[183] For I am *persuaded*, that neither death, nor life, nor angels, nor principalities, nor powers, nor things present, nor things to come, Nor height, nor depth, nor any other creature, shall be able to separate us from the love of God, which is in Christ Jesus our Lord. (Romans 8:38).

all "*bible*" translations as "*Versions*" *[**re-**Versions]*. The *Received Text Bible (KJB)* is *NOT* just another "Version", but ***the** Only* Word of God in English.

The Luciferians want it to "appear" that they "***re-**Imagined*" that there is no difference between any of the other 1,000+ Luciferian "*Versions*" *[**re-**Versions]* and the *Received Text **Bible***. *God is furious and curses all those who would **per-**Vert His Word!*[184]

This conflict is not a "*King James* Only" Controversy. This is more accurately identified as the "*Westcott & Hort Only*" *Controversy*!

This implies that all of these 1,000+ demonically corrupted "Versions" *[**re-**Versions]* are rooted in the same original "bible" text, and from the same source as the *Received Text Bible*. *Webster's Dictionary* defines "*Version*" as:

> ...an account or description *from a particular point of view* especially as *contrasted* with another account, *another version*.

A "*Version*" is biased to "*a particular point of view*". A "*Version*" *[**re-**Version]* takes the original and makes it *different* in *contrast* to the *original*. By U.S. copywrite law, *it is required that each "Version" [**re-**Version] differs from all other Versions [**re-**Version] thousands of times*. As codified in the Law of Physics, and God's inerrant Word *demands*, *Things that are different, are NOT the same!*

These ***per-**Verters* naturally refer to the *King James Bible*, as the *King James "Version"*. Do you see their sleight of hand? The *Received Text*

[184] Which is not another; but there be some that trouble you, and would pervert the gospel of Christ. But though we, or an angel from heaven, preach any other gospel unto you than that which we have preached unto you, let him be accursed. As we said before, so say I now again, If any man preach any other gospel unto you than that ye have received, let him be accursed. (Galatians 1:7-9).

Bible (*KJB*) is the only *Word of God* in English, from which all other "*Versions*" *[**re-**Versions]* are intentionally corrupted and ***per-****Verted*. Also, it should be noted that the only people calling the *King James Version* are those who stand against the KJB, the "*Westcott & Hort Only*" *Conspirators* as discussed in the following chapter: *17.1. The "Westcott & Hort Only" Controversy*.

Stay with God's Only Word, the *King James Standardized Bible* and you will be aligned with God!

Book Notes

17.1. The "Westcott & Hort Only" Controversy...

The "Westcott & Hort Only" Controversy...
I Believe that collective Christianity has passively allowed the "*King James* Only" Controversy to be *misbranded*... When it is actually a "*Westcott & Hort Only*" *Controversy*...

There has been a great divide created in the Church over which "'*bible' Version*" *[**re-**Version]* is the true Word of GOD. We know that *there can only be One GOD inspired Bible translation* in each language, otherwise GOD would be schizophrenic, deceptive, and even a liar. **No! *GOD Forbid!***

Did GOD give His Word, in a thousand different contradicting ways *[**re-**Versions]*, to a thousand different people *[**re-**Writers]*, and a thousand different publishing houses [***re-**Proofs*], with a thousand opposing copyrights *[**re-**Righters]*, so you could cherry-pick whatever "*Version*" *[**re-**Version]* you "*feel*" fits your personal *emotional theology* test? ***No! GOD Forbid!***[185]

GOD does *not* allow anyone to mix and match His words; GOD has *One* Word that is preserved *[**pre-**Served]* forever for Eternity![186] No sane, nor rational person can talk out of a thousand different sides their mouth, in tens-of-thousands of different contradictions, claiming it's all GOD's Word of Truth. Satan is hard at work to destroy GOD's one-and-only True *Bible* (*KJB)*!

This is exactly what happens because *every* "'bible' *Version*" *[**re-**Version]* is a *contradiction to all others*. *Contradictions* in *tens-of-thousands of different places and ways*. **This is *the very definition of Satan induced spiritual schizophrenic insanity***!

185 What shall we say then? Is there unrighteousness with God? God forbid. (Romans 9:14).
186 Psalms 119:160; Isaiah 40:8; 1 Peter 1:24.

(Of course, if GOD were schizophrenic, deceptive, or even a liar, GOD then would not be GOD at all... and that is the point of the Luciferians, to eliminate GOD! These Luciferian "'bible' *Versions*" *[**re-**Versions]* are *intentionally* plagued with Luciferian ***re-**Translations*, ***re-**Versions*, *contra-dictions*, and *Lies*! And remember... *GOD cannot lie*[187].)

Remember that *JESUS is the Logos Word, the literal written Word of GOD*. JESUS embodies and *IS* the written Word of GOD.[188] JESUS "is the same yesterday, to day, and for ever."

The True Word of GOD will *never* change, just as JESUS can *never* change. The Word of GOD is *NEVER* a plurality, there is only One singular Word of GOD in each language, settled forever in Heaven":

> *For ever*, O LORD, thy word is *settled* in heaven.
> (Psalms 119:89)

The *Received Text Bible* (*KJB*) is the Original, Eternal, and only *Word of GOD* in English. So, it *cannot* be a "*King James* Only" Controversy. It is a Controversy of the interlopers who try to *reinvent* GOD's Word according to their own Evil bias making it a "*Westcott & Hort Only*" *Controversy*! GOD tells us very clearly that those preaching, teaching, or studying "another gospel", other than the Word of GOD are Cursed by GOD![189]

How is it that those who promote "another gospel" *Versions [**re-**Versions]* always agree with all the 1,000+ *Versions [**re-**Versions]*,

---

[187] Titus 1:2.

[188] Search the *scriptures*; for in them ye think ye have eternal life: and *they are they which testify of me*. (John 5:39); 10:34; Hebrews 10:7.

[189] I marvel that ye are so soon removed from him that called you into the grace of Christ unto another gospel: Which is not another; but there be some that trouble you, and would pervert the gospel of Christ. But though we, or an angel from heaven, preach any other gospel unto you than that which we have preached unto you, let him be accursed. As we said before, so say I now again, If any man preach any other gospel unto you than that ye have received, let him be accursed. (Galatians 1:6-9).

all except, of course, the *Received Text Bible* (*KJB*)? They do so exactly as the Luciferians Westcott, Hort, Strong, and Blavatsky *Confederacy* had plotted, against the "christian churches". Many which have now been infiltrated the churches formerly of GOD, have become *Luciferian Lodges* unbeknownst to most in the pews.

Think about that for a minute... You know a person by the friends they keep... *like their friend Lucifer!* It is a *Controversy* of those who want to follow an intentionally corrupted "'bible' *Version*" *[**re-**Version]*.[190] This is a man-made, and Satan encouraged license to sin!

The *Received Text Bible* (*KJB*) was the ***only*** accepted English language *Bible* as "*Received*" from the First Day of Pentecost originating over 2,200 years ago. These modern "*Westcott & Hort Only*" interlopers would have you believe that GOD had it all wrong for some 2,000+ years, and their "*Versions*" *[**re-**Versions]*, of formerly "Secret Knowledge"[191], [192] are better than what the Christian Church *Received from GOD*! ***Not a good place to make your stand!***

Schizophrenia and the *Westcott & Hort* "***re-**Versions*":
From a clinical standpoint, only a *schizophrenic* defends multiple *contradictory* statements at the same time. This *spiritual schizophrenia* is inherent in all of the 1,000+ "alternate 'bible' *Versions*" *[**re-**Versions]*, which then becomes an insurmountable dilemma for the "*Westcott & Hort Only*" *Controversy* crowd, a position that they *cannot* reasonably defend: [193]

---

[190] Be not deceived: evil communications corrupt good manners. (1 Corinthians 15:33).
[191] For a full discussion of "secret knowledge" see: el Yerak, Dr. Rhema; JESUS and JEHOVAH or Yeshua and Yahweh; What Difference Does It Make What We Call GOD and His Son Anyway? Advanced Level Edition.
[192] El Yerak, Dr. Rhema; WALKING BY FAITH... What Is Faith, How To Live By Faith, and Finally Living the Victorious Christian Life!; Advanced Level Edition.
[193] See: el Yerak, Dr. Rhema; The Left's War Against GOD!: and The Right's Rules for Anti-Radicals!; A Call to Action!; Volume 01; Master Level Edition. The Left Is a RELIGION!; Opening Quote.

He, who will not reason is a bigot;
he who cannot, is a fool;
and he, who dares not, is a slave!

A Rule of Logic states that: *Things that are different are not the same*, or also called a "false equivalence", or a "logical fallacy", a form of *spiritual schizophrenia*. It is a violation of this unassailable Scientific Law as set by GOD. This is a "False Equivalence" based on "Unreasonable Comparisons" *[**re-**Versions]* are *spiritually schizophrenic*. ***Evil makes you stupid!***[194]

In fact, being "*unreasonable*" and "*illogical*" are the foundational definitions of *insanity*. Whether in religion or politics, all liberals are by definition, *illogical*, and *unreasonable*, being *spiritually schizophrenic*.[195]

The Essence of the Westcott & Hort Only "scheme"[196] was to Erase JESUS from the *Bible* and then Replace JESUS, with Lucifer!
This is the principal reason why many people today say that "the '*Bible*' cannot be trusted because of all of its errors and 'contradictions'". This doubt is actually *logically* triggered in their minds by the *thousands* of conflicts within, *and between*, *all* the

[194] See especially the author's Book: el Yerak, Dr. Rhema; The Left's War Against GOD!: and The Right's Rules for Anti-Radicals!; A Call to Action!; The Left Is a RELIGION!; Volume 01; Master Level Edition; pp 201.
[195] False equivalence is a logical fallacy that occurs when someone incorrectly asserts that two or more things are equivalent, simply because they share some characteristics, despite the fact that there are also notable differences between them. Accordingly, false equivalences are frequently used in debates on various topics, especially when it comes to suggesting that there is a moral equivalence between two or more things that are being equated. The equivalence exaggerates the importance of the similarity between the things being equated, it ignores important differences between the things being equated, and ignores differences in orders of magnitude between the things being equated; *False Equivalence: The Problem with Unreasonable Comparisons*; https://effectiviology.com/false-equivalence/.
[196] For "scheme" see "*Back to Westcott & Hort...*" below.

1,000+ corrupted Westcott & Hort translation deviations *[**re-**Versions]*.

It seems a bit schizophrenic to me that so many preachers quote from several *different* Westcott & Hort Only based "'bible' *Versions*" *[**re-**Versions]*, in the same sermon or article. This is the very definition of ***spiritual schizophrenia, for which the healthy, natural mind cannot rightly or logically reconcile***. GOD is not the author of confusion[197], whereas Satan is the source of all *confusion*[198]. Remember that *schizophrenia is a form of insanity*. In this case, *spiritual schizophrenic insanity*[199]. (The Luciferian references are explained below.)

I discovered ***GOD's Bible Picture Puzzle Study Method***™ over a decades-long deep-dive *Bible Study*. There is a cost to everything and... *You gotta want it!*

Most Christians would not pay the horrific price to receive this kind of remarkable revelation. Looking back, I do not think that I would voluntarily chosen this path and the horrific cost it bears. But after having already paid the price, I feel Blessed that GOD trusted me with such a heavy burden borne over decades. Thank You GOD...

Remember also that, in spiritual terms, *schizophrenia* is not actually a simple clinical diagnosis, but *spiritual schizophrenic insanity is the* ***conflicting voices of devils inside the same mind***.

Same Devils, Different Names! We are commanded by GOD to *not* try to make the *Bible* say what we want... we are to conform[200] ourselves by the Holy Spirit to "*What Does GOD Say?*" in His Word.

These are the devils Doing the Devil's Work!

---

197 1 Corinthians 14:33.

198 James 3:16.

199 Jeremiah 50:38; Luke 6:11.

200 Romans 12:2.

A note here: The *Received Text Bible (KJB)* stands alone as the *only* English *Bible, and as such,* it has absolutely *NO* contradictions within its pages... *None*! I have spent decades and thousands of hours intensely studying the *Received Text Bible* (*KJB*) and there is *not one single contradiction in it...*

➢➢ ANYONE who Identifies as a "Bible Critic" is Criticizing God and is NOT a Christian! ⮘⮘

The "contradiction" [*contra-dictions*] problem only comes when "*Bible* critics" try to compare any of the "*Westcott & Hort Luciferian Versions*" *[**re-**Versions]* back into another corrupted English "Version" *[**re-re-**Version]*.

"*Bible*" contradictions [*contra-dictions*] *ONLY* exist outside of *The Received Text Bible* (*KJB*). Men's minds are logical, and evil corrupts the God-given logical mind into an evil mind ruled by *emotion*. Satan did not go to Adam first and reason with Adam about sinning.

Satan went to Eve where Satan weaved an *emotional* challenge to God's Word where logic and reason were summarily suspended. Suspended, in order for Eve to *rationalize* away her sin. Reasoning is Logical based on the intrinsic facts; *Rationalization is being led and controlled by feelings and emotions.*

God's very nature is Reasonable,[201] and therefore Logical, a trait that God tells His children to follow. There is another Law of Logic, the *Law of Non-Contradiction*, which states that "*contradictory propositions cannot both be true in the same sense at the same time*".

---

[201] Come now, and let us *reason* together, saith the Lord [God Jehovah] (Isaiah 1:18).

This is another unanswerable logical dilemma for Luciferian liberals and critics: ***All*** 1,000+ Luciferian based *Westcott & Hort* "'bible' *Versions*" *[**re-**Versions]*, contradict ***ALL*** other *Westcott & Hort* "*Versions*" *[**re-**Versions]*... in *tens-of-thousands* of places.

Given *the Law of Non-Contradiction, ONLY One "translation" of the Bible can be True in each language*, and *that One in* English is *The Received Text Bible (KJB)* where there are ***no*** contradictions. The chain of custody can be traced all the way back to the First New Testament Day of Pentecost.[202]

The *Received Text Bible* (*KJB*) supporters will sit and reason with others on the differences between the *Received Text Bible* (*KJB*) and the other "*Versions*" *[**re-**Versions]*. The LORD God says to Believers "come let us reason together"[203]. The opponents of the *Received Text Bible* (*KJB*) have emotionally and maliciously maligned and attacked GOD's "*Received Text Bible* (*KJB*)", and especially the supporters of *The Received Text Bible* (*KJB*).

Whether it be politics or religion, this is *always* a tactic of Evil ungodly Leftists[204] to try to label you as something that isn't true. In this, they *deflect* and project their own guilt for doing *exactly* what they accuse you of doing! These arrogant "*Westcott & Hort Only*" "'bible' critics" openly and exclusively mock the *Received Text Bible* (*KJB*) and its adherents from the pulpit.[205] GOD Save their souls!

When you stand behind the pulpit and speak, you are literally declaring, "Thus saith the LORD"! GOD will deal very harshly in Eternity

202 See following Chapter: Appendix 5- Lineage of the Received Text, Textus Receptus, King James Bible (KJB) from Day of Pentecost to Today.

203 Isaiah 1:18.

204 For the terms Right and Left as Biblical terms see: el Yerak, Dr. Rhema; The Left's War Against GOD!: and The Right's Rules for Anti-Radicals!; A Call to Action!; Volume 01; Master Level Edition; chapter: Defining The War: Evil Against GOD, Left Against Right.

205 el Yerak, Dr. Rhema; The Left's War Against GOD!: and The Right's Rules for Anti-Radicals!; A Call to Action!; Volume 01; Master Level Edition; Pages 89, 100, 126, 154.

with those people who *falsely* claim Satan's words as God's Word.[206]

With Liberals it is always their *emotion*, verses God's Reason. I have seen this many, many times, usually in a totally off-topic moment, where the preacher from the pulpit openly mocks The *Received Text Bible* (*KJB*) advocates and *The Received Text* (*KJB*) itself.

In this, it literally appears as if a devil whispers in the preacher's ear and they dutifully obey. Jesus says that half of the people in church are pretenders and going straight to Hell.[207] I bet you did not hear that from the pulpit!

Humm... you know a person by their fruit. This fruit is Eve's putrid apple that looks appealing on the outside, but contains damnation in the bite! This includes the Preacher and administrative staff. Be very careful who you follow... Tough words, but spoken in Truth.

These interlopers will be eternally Cursed[208]. They will be cursed for speaking and quoting from the conflicting Luciferian "'bible' *Versions*"[209] *[**re-**Versions]*. God is the one and only source of Truth[210].

(There is a point to be made here. If you are a bit overcome by the repeated use of the phrase "*[**re-**Versions]*", in its various forms, imagine God's anger at Luciferians 1,000+ repeated mockeries of God's True Word...)

I have *never* heard a preacher from the pulpit stop the service to mock any of the other *1,000+* "Versions". A tell-tale is in Utah, a

---

206 My brethren, be not many masters, knowing that we shall receive the greater condemnation. (James 3:1).
207 Matthew 25:1-13.
208 Galatians 1:8-9; 3:1-5.
209 Deuteronomy 18:20; Jeremiah 14:15-16; 23:11-12, 16; 23:15, 21; 29:31-32.
210 Jesus saith unto him, I am the way, the truth, and the life: no man cometh unto the Father, but by me. (John 14:6).

school district banned the *Bible*… but only the *Received Text Bible* (*KJB*). *Isn't that curious?* All of the other Luciferian ***re-****Versions* were welcomed. Satan knows the difference… do you?

The *only* *"Bible"* the Devil hates, attacks, mocks, and derides is *The Received Text Bible* (*KJB*). You know a person by the company they keep[211]… and the Devil is best friends with the "*Westcott & Hort Only*" *Conspiracy* crowd.

"*Westcott & Hort Only*" *Deception* and *Deflection*:
The bottom line is that the so-called "*King James* Only" *propaganda* of the religious Liberals, is in reality a "*Westcott & Hort Only*" *deception* and *deflection*. This "*Westcott & Hort Only*" crowd is totally and singularly opposed *only* to the *Received Text Bible* (*KJB*), while *ANY* of the other 1,000+ *Westcott & Hort* chain translations they enthusiastically endorse.

The Received Text Bible (*KJB*) has stood ***un***challenged for over *1,900+ years*, and these *Westcott & Hort Only* horde have only been around for about 150 years. John Hinton of Harvard University notes:

> *Suggestions to alter the text is a common method of attacking the Bible* that has been employed by Bible-scoffing scholars in academia for over 100 years, it is a common practice that I encountered frequently among fellow students in Hebrew classes. The practice is taught and encouraged by those who consider the Bible to be *mythology*.[212]

Did GOD let an uninspired *Bible* go uncorrected for 1,900+ years? While waiting for His *Holy Word* to be "*corrected*" by a group of *self-identified* Luciferians, like Westcott, Hort, and Strong? *GOD forbid!* *The Received Text Bible* (*KJB*) Believers stand on an accepted 2,200-year-old *Received Text Bible* (*KJB*).

---

[211] Be not deceived: evil communications corrupt good manners. (1 Corinthians 15:33).
[212] Hinton, John, Ph.D., Harvard University; Ridiculous KJV Bible Corrections: Who is Yahweh?

Whereas the "*Westcott & Hort Only*" Confederacy stands on the stacks of "***re***-*Imagined*"[213] 100-year-old ***re-re***-*Translated* Luciferian "'bible' *Versions*" [***re***-*Versions*]; These "'bible' *Versions*" are actually not retranslations, but "***re***-*Interpretations*" *from their Luciferian religious dogmata founded and forged in the fires of Hell by Westcott & Hort and other plethora of the Devil's minions*.

The fact is that Westcott & Hort began with The *Received Text Bible* (*KJB*) New Testament, and then *intentionally deconstructed* [***re***-*Verted*] it to "*quietly*"[214] ***re***-Create their new ***re***-*Imagined*, falsified, and demonically ***de***-*Constructed, then* ***re***-*Constructed Luciferian* " new" "***Greek New Testament***".

There are extant letters between *Westcott & Hort* discussing their Luciferian conspiracy to ***de***-*Construct* the *Received Text Bible (KJB)* and replace it with a Luciferian reconstruct. A "new" *Greek New Testament*, which they carefully ***re***-*aligned* with their Luciferian philosophies as the Luciferian Blavatsky horde predesigned. These are evil men who worship the creature[215] Satan, and not the Creator GOD.

Then *Westcott & Hort* used their own newly and intentionally corrupted new "Greek New Testament" and ***re-re***-*Translated* it into their new Luciferian "*Revised Version* 'bible'" [***re***-*Versioned* "bible"].

---

[213] Because that, when they knew God, they glorified him not as God, neither were thankful; but became vain in their imaginations, and their foolish heart was darkened. Professing themselves to be wise, they became fools, (Romans 1:21-22).
[214] Life and letters of Fenton John Anthony Hort, Vol. 1, 1896, p. 400.
[215] Who changed the truth of God into a lie, and worshipped and served the creature more than the Creator, who is blessed for ever. Amen. (Romans 1:25).

Again, it begs the bigger question: Would GOD leave the world without a dependable, inerrant, pure and word-for-word *Bible* for 2,000+ years?[216] (Hint: *No way in Hell!*[217])

Not the GOD of *The Received Text Bible* (*KJB*). Only evil men and devils playing "god" would dare to "***re-****Interpret*" [***re-****Version*] GOD's Eternal, literal, and unchanging *Word*.[218]

Why Is the *Received Text Bible* (*KJB*) the *Only Bible* "translation" Attacked?

It was only after I committed to wholeheartedly *Study* the *Bible* that I began to really read the *Bible* to understand it. Don't misunderstand, I have compared dozens of other "'bible' *Versions*" [***re-****Versions*] to the *Received Text Bible* (*KJB*). From the intentional omissions and additions in these *Westcott & Hort Only* Heathenisms, the Spirit in my spirit *always* led me back to *The Received Text Bible* (*KJB*).

I also knew intuitively that the *Received Text Bible* (*KJB*) was the only *Bible* that I could use. *The Received Text Bible (KJB) was the only translation that had the Power of GOD upon it,*[219] *and JESUS as Savior in it*. I could literally sense the *Power* and *Presence* of GOD flowing through this *Bible* (KJB). It was attacked by the atheist, and apostate "Christian" crowd alike. Again, you know a person by the friends they keep, and who they identify as their enemies.

[216] Every word of God is pure: he is a shield unto them that put their trust in him. (Proverbs 30:5).

[217] Yes, the use of the word "Hell" is intentional. As in born in the Pits of Hell.

[218] Genesis 3:1-6; Matthew chapter Luke chapter 4.

[219] Hinton, John, Ph.D., Harvard University; Ridiculous KJV Bible Corrections: Who is Yahweh?

➢➢ ANYONE who Identifies as a "Bible Critic" is NOT a Christian! ➣➣

A *Bible* Challenge...
On one occasion I was challenged by a self-identified "Messianic Jew"[220] who was sincerely seeking after God. He challenged me that if I could show him 3 places in the *Bible* where Jesus is called God, then he would gladly submit himself to Jesus as his God and Savior.

I thought that that was the easiest challenge I had ever been offered! I presented him with ten Scriptures where Jesus is clearly called God. However, it had been blotted out of his *Westcott & Hort* "'bible' *Version*" [***re-****Version*] Luciferian translation.

I did this every day for almost three weeks amounting to hundreds of verses. *Every* passage I presented in the New and Old Testaments that showed Jesus as God in the *Received Text Bible* (*KJB*), was adulterated in his *Westcott & Hort New International Version* (NIV) [***re-****Version*].

I was stunned to discover that *EVERY* reference to Jesus as God had been *intentionally* carved out in his NIV. When he decided to "try" studying *The Received Text Bible* (*KJB*), he quickly found the True God for the first time, and gave his life to Jesus as his God and Savior! *Amen!* He finally found Salvation in Jesus that he had diligently been seeking! That is the *Power* of God to quicken his soul only found in the *King James Bible*.

[220] I am an actual Messianic Jew. A Messianic Jew is a Christian of Jewish descent who acknowledges Jesus as the Jewish Messiah, and has accepted Jesus as their God and Savior. This self-identified Messianic Jew in his demonic confusion had settled falsely on this moniker. Remember that there is no Salvation in the Old Testament.

Salvation is only in the *Received Text King James Bible*. All other "*Versions*" [***re-****Versions*] were derived from the corrupted Westcott & Hort's Luciferian variants, where JESUS as GOD had been wholly and utterly erased.

Back to the *Westcott & Hort* Scheme...

> In 1853, F.J.A. Hort and B.F. Westcott agreed, upon the suggestion of publisher Daniel Macmillan, to take part in "*an interesting and comprehensive 'New Testament Scheme*,'" that is, to undertake *a joint **revision*** [***re-****Versions*] *of the Greek New Testament*. ***The project was withheld from public knowledge during the twenty years required by Westcott and Hort to complete the New Greek Text*** and during the subsequent ten years during which an English Revision Committee "revised" the 1682 Authorized Version[221] (*KJB*) to their matching *corrupt* *Revised Version* (RV) [***re****-Version*].

This "*Scheme*" as MacMillan identified it, ***was not*** "*a joint **revision*** [***re-****Version*] *of the Greek New Testament"*, but *deconstruction* and *corruption* of the English *The Received Text Bible (KJB)*. By their *secret scheme* having "*withheld from public knowledge"*, Westcott & Hort could corrupt the English *Received Text Bible* (*KJB*) that had stood unchallenged for 2,000+ years.

Wescott & Hort used their "newly" *corrupted* Greek New Testament ***re****-Version* to then **re-*re*-***Translate* a whole "new" English New Testament ***Revised "Version" [re-Version]***. Which is *to **re**-Vert from the King James Bible, to the Westcott & Hort Revised "Greek" [**re**-Vert] "Version", and **re-re**-Vert it again into their English* Revised Version *abomination* [***re****-Abomination*]. Yes, it's as ugly as it sounds. This Revised "*Version*" *[**re**-Version]* was wholly drawn from their own "Greek" corruptions in accordance with their "New Age" and Luciferian beliefs.

221 *Bible* Ready; *Westcott And Hort*; https://www.bibleready.org/westcott-and-hort.

> ... the text of Westcott and Hort is followed in all essentials... I think with pleasure of the preacher or teacher who under the inspiration of this Grammar may turn afresh to his *Greek* New Testament and there find things new and old, the vital message all electric with power for the new age[222]

Bishop Brooke Foss Westcott and Dr. Fenton John Anthony Hort were active members of Madam Helena Blavatsky's *Theosophical Society* (Theosophy is the worship of *Lucifer* as their god.) and supporters of Blavatsky's ***Lucifer Magazine***.

Helena Petrovna Blavatsky

Helena Petrovna Blavatsky was an *Occultist* who *worshipped Lucifer*; founded the Theosophic Society; published the *Lucifer Magazine*; was a *Cabalist*; followed the Hermetic Society (the worship of the Luciferian Baphomet god shown below); and as noted previously in this chapter, developed the plan "*to infiltrate Christian Churches and subtilty convert them to Luciferian Lodges*".

Terrifyingly, this is what the majority of "churches" today who follow the *Westcott & Hort Only Corruptions* have literally become...

[222] A.T. Robertson, *A Grammar of the Greek New Testament in the Light of Historical Research*, Hodder & Stoughton, George H. Doran, 1934, p. 12 [Original at Indiana University]

Luciferian Lodges![223] Whether they follow Lucifer by ignorance, or intention, it matters not to GOD.

Ignorance Is No Excuse ...

The Baphomet statue, is the Satanic Pagan Representation of Lucifer as "god"...

The Baphomet
Knights Templar 1098 A.D.

The Baphomet
Satanic Temple Today

Hermes is another name for Satan who is androgynous (the mythology having both male and female genitalia as the above images reveal.), and will present himself as a homosexual through the coming Antichrist.[224] *Did you ever wonder why the Leftist GOD-haters' most sacred doctrine is homosexuality?*

---

[223] Not all apostates realize their transformation to Luciferianism. Many naturally transition to Luciferianism because of a haughty spirit of arrogance, but are led away by a devil spirit nonetheless. "Pride goeth before destruction, and an haughty spirit before a fall." (Proverbs 16:18).

[224] Neither shall he regard the God of his fathers, *nor the desire of women*, nor regard any god: for he shall magnify himself above all. (Daniel 11:37).

Clubs founded by *Westcott & Hort* were noted for the intensity of the *homosexual* relations between its members, and especially the young male students. Remember also, considering the picture above on the upper right, that the worship of Lucifer from the beginning of time has always involved child sacrifice[225].
Westcott & Hort were also founding members of the *Ghostly Guild*. The *Ghostly Guild* held regular séances, practiced necromancy[226], and conjured up devil spirits. *Westcott & Hort* also formed a club called *"The Hermes Club"* at Cambridge College named after the Graeco-Egyptian Pagan "god", *Hermes Trismegistus,*[227] who is Lucifer. *The Knights Templar worshiped the Baphomet as a representation of Satan with full homosexual rites*.[228] (See Image above)

Fellow ***Re****vised* ***Version*** ***[re****-Version]* "bible" *Committee* member and homosexual C. J. Vaughan, was a director at Harrow school for boys, ages 13 to 18, and was *dismissed for homosexual conduct with the young male students; these young male students were directly* ***in the charge of B.F. Westcott***. At Harrow school for boys Westcott and several other administrators held violent homosexual orgies for which there were a number of complaints made by some of the younger male students.

Westcott & Hort followed their Luciferian predispositions against the *Received Text Bible* (*KJB*) and *deconstructed* the New Testament of the *Received Text Bible* "back" into Greek, then ***re-re-****Translating* it back into English, deceivingly creating a "new" Greek New Testament [***re****-Version]*. All the while, each feigned to have studiously labored

[225] el Yerak, Dr. Rhema; Jesus and Jehovah or Yeshua and Yahweh; What Difference Does It Make What We Call God and His Son Anyway? Advanced Level Edition.
[226] Sex with the dead.
[227] Alan Gauld, *The Founders of Psychical Research* (New York: Schocken Books, 1968), pp. 90-91.
[228] See the Knights Templar and the Baphomet in the above left picture.

for twenty years to "fix the errors" they pretended existed in the *Received Text Bible (KJB),* which as stated had stood unchallenged for 2,000+ years.

Westcott & Hort *"changed the Truth of God into a lie" adding* to *their* New Greek New Testament *such corruptions as removing the sin of sodomy*[229] (homosexuality); *removing the GODhead of JESUS; denying the GODhead of the Holy Spirit; removing Hell* as a literal place of eternal punishment; *promoted a "works" based "salvation"* thereby *eliminating JESUS' blood atonement; and equated Lucifer and JESUS as the same disembodied being!* All from the deepest recesses of Hell...

How these devils did the Devil's work... *in the Dark*:
Westcott & Hort *"deconstructed"* the New Testament of The *Received Text Bible* (*KJB*) "back" into the "New" Greek New Testament, and then *"reconstructed"* this *abomination* back into the English ***Revised Version [re-Version]*** "bible". This is the "bridge" to the ***Revised Version*** Committee, *including James Strong,* who then used the corrupted Wescott & Hort *Greek New Testament* to "***re-re-Translate***" ***[re-re-Version]*** the "New Testament" back to English and insert these abominations into his *Strong's "Exhaustive Concordance of the Bible".*

In 1885, the "New" ***Revised Version [re-Version]*** (RV) Luciferian "bible" was published. The corrupted "New" *Greek New Testament* was the foundation upon which the ***Revised*** Version "bible" was "***re-re-Translated***" ***[re-re-Versioned]*** back into English. Yes, that can be a bit difficult to follow, but remember that the agents of the Devil use shrouds, misdirection, secrecy, and confusion to conceal their machinations of Evil. GOD's Word exposes this method of blasphemy as, "beguiled, subtility, and corruption".[230]

---

[229] GOD tells us that sodomy, homosexuality, is the worst of all sins. Once the homosexual devil spirit moves into a non-christian, ALL the other devils come in also. Romans (1:24-32).
[230] 2 Corinthians 11:3.

Hort was fearful of being found out in their Luciferian "***re-re-****Translation*":

> 1861: Apr. 12th - Hort to Westcott: "Also - but this may be cowardice - I have a sort of craving that our text should be cast upon the world before we deal with matters likely to brand us with ***suspicion***. *I mean, a text, issued by* ***men already known for*** (Luciferianism, homosexuality, etc.) and then what will undoubtedly be treated as **dangerous *heresy***, will have great difficulties in finding its way to regions which it might otherwise hope to reach, and *whence it would not be easily banished by subsequent alarms*."[231]

Here is an excellent summation of the characters of Westcott & Hort:

> Philo of Alexandria [Luciferian texts] would have been proud of Westcott and Hort's *allegorizing*, *spiritualizing*, and *pontificating*. For the rest of us, who just want to read God's Word instead of *intellectual balderdash*; I say thank the Lord for the internet *so that these two elitist cancers can finally be radiated with light*.[232]

James Strong:

*Strong's Exhaustive Concordance of the Revised Version [****re-****Version]* "bible"...

James Strong is most recognized for his *"Strong's Exhaustive Concordance of the Bible"* published in 1880, and regrettably, it still stands as the most nefarious Christian reference book to date.

Unfortunately for Christians, Strong was *not* a Christian, but a *Luciferian* whose extent infiltration targeted Church "theology". This infiltration of the true Church, as advocated by his contemporary Luciferian Helena Blavatsky, has retroactively turned much of

[231] Westcott, Arthur; *Life and Letters of Brooke Foss Westcott*; New York; 1903; Vol. 1, p. 445.

[232] *Bible Ready*; *Westcott And Hort*; https://www.bibleready.org/westcott-and-hort.

Christendom into *Luciferian Lodges*. And most Christians remain ignorant of this subtile heresy!

Here is an accurate, albeit painful, quote that best sums up the damage that James Strong's Luciferian infiltration has caused for the Church and Christians:

> *James Strong* (1822-1894), author of *Strong's Concordance*, *has been elevated to the position of* ***fourth member of the Trinity by many***. *His corrupt Greek and Hebrew definitions pepper today's preaching,* ***as if his lexicon was the final and 67th book of the Bible***.[233]
>
> [G.A.] Riplinger also points out that the early ***re***-*Version* [author emphasis] of the name of God (Yahweh) was used by a Catholic in the fifth century who did not know Hebrew by the name of Theodoret who confused it with a Syrian Jabe. (*The New Schaff-Herzog Encyclopedia of Religious Knowledge*, Vol. XI). Later, prominent atheist scholars such as Driver of Brown, Driver and Briggs Hebrew Dictionary fame (the text that James Strong plagiarized for his concordance's dictionary), *proposed connections with deities from Aramaic and Babylonian texts* named Yaho, Ya-hu, or Yave.[234]

James Strong was a member of the *Luciferian Society*, promoted a *One World government*, a *One World religion with Lucifer* at its Head, *denied the deity of JESUS Christ*, ***had a seat on the Revised Version (RV) [re-Version] Bible translating committee*** with Westcott & Hort, *denied the Personhood of the Holy Spirit, denounced the inerrancy of the "Bible"*, taught that much of the Old Testament was "***metaphorical***" and not literal, *promoted Evolution, did not believe in a literal Hell, supported the Koran as equal to the Christian Bible*, was an *anti-Semite* (hated Jews), *denied that GOD directly inspired the*

---

[233] GA Riplinger; *Hazardous Materials*; P. 162.

[234] Hinton, John, Ph.D., Harvard University; Ridiculous KJV Bible Corrections: Who is Yahweh?

Scriptures[235], and equated Lucifer and JESUS Christ as the same person! A resumé from the Pit of Hell!

ONLY a true Christian, by the Indwelling of the Holy Spirit, can Correctly Discern *Biblical* Text.[236]
Many who claim to be Christians are, according to the *JESUS*, not Christians, but Luciferians possessed by devil spirits. Unbelievers, and too many Christians use the wrong "spirit" to twist the Scriptures to match their heretical and evil motivations. GOD tells Believers to:

> ... *try the spirits whether they are of God*: ***because many false prophets are gone out into the world***. (1 John 4:1)
>
> But *the natural man receiveth not the things of the Spirit of God*: for *they are foolishness unto him: neither can he know them, because they are spiritually discerned*. (1 Corinthians 2:14).

Westcott, Hort, and Strong collaborated with others on the *RV Committee* to create the ***Revised*** Version (RV) ***[re-Version]*** ***re-re-****Interpretation*, which was ***falsified*** as the first non-Papist "*Version*", and stood wholly opposed to *The Received Text Bible* (*KJB*).

The "***Reviser's***" ***[re-****Versionists]* first task was to construct the Greek text... for which the Revisers were *privately* supplied with installments of Westcott & Hort's text..."[237]. (Notice that everything associated with Evil is a *scheme* that is: secret, hidden, private, withheld from public knowledge, in the dark, *et al*) Westcott & Hort [and Strong] had *changed approximately 9,970 words* from the

---

[235] All scripture is given by inspiration of God, and is profitable for doctrine, for reproof, for correction, for instruction in righteousness: (2 Timothy 3:16).
[236] 1 Corinthians 2:10-14.
[237] *Encyclopedia Britannica*; 1911; vol. 3, p. 903.

traditional Greek New Testament[238] (the New Testament of *The Received Text Bible* (*KJB*)).

Things that are different are not the same!

This "new" RV *[**re**-Version]* translation incorporated all of Westcott & Hort's Luciferian influences, which not by coincidence, then matched the *Strong's Exhaustive Concordance of the Bible*. Strong's system of asterisks in his *Concordance* leads to many accepting the corresponding *Westcott & Hort Revised Version's [**re**-Version's]* corrupted and Luciferian word choices. As the Jewish Cabalists erasing the Hebrew vowel points[239], so as to ***re-re***-*Translate* any Hebrew text at will and transforming it to a *"**new**" intentionally **per**-Version "Version" [**re**-Version]*.

One must be *very careful* in handling the *Strong's Exhaustive Concordance of the Bible*! Strong used *subtile*[240] tricks designed to deceive the reader. Strong very subtly used 2 different type fonts in defining *Bible* words.

I discovered this deception for myself in extensively using *Strong's Concordance*. The actual *Received Text Bible* definitions are in 'standard type', whereas the ***re***-Defined *Westcott & Hort* Luciferian definitions Strong employed an *'italic type'*.

These *cleverly disguised* differences can easily pass wholly unnoticed. Too often people assume that *all* the definitions in *Strong's Concordance* are legitimate "*Bible* definitions". They are *NOT*!

---

[238] GA Riplinger; *Hazardous Materials*; P. 168.

[239] el Yerak, Dr. Rhema; JESUS and JEHOVAH or Yeshua and Yahweh; What Difference Does It Make What We Call GOD and His Son Anyway? Advanced Level Edition.

[240] But I fear, lest by any means, as the serpent beguiled Eve through his *subtilty*, so your minds should be corrupted from the *simplicity* that is in Christ. (2 Corinthians 11:3).

Using Strong's deceptive *"italic"* cypher system, Strong changed *God's Holy Word* into a Luciferian ***re-re-****Interpretation* *[****re-re-****Version]*. The real *Bible* definitions are laid out side-by-side with the Luciferian *italicized* definitions giving the impression that are all equally *Biblical "Versions"*. **They are *NOT!***

The disclosure of this deception is cleverly buried and coded in the "SIGNS EMPLOYED" section stated in *Strong's Concordance* deceivingly as:

> *Italics*, at the end of a rendering from the A.V. (*Authorized Version, King James Bible*), denote an explanation of the *variations [****re-****Variations]* from the usual form.

One must almost be a studied linguist to decode the language Strong hides behind here. In plain English, this is my suggested *Truth*:

> All definitions in *"italics"* are intentionally sabotaged by Strong to fit his Luciferian definitions and *NOT* an actual part of *The Received Text Bible* (*KJB*) definitions.

This is evidentially reflected in the corrupt *"Revised Version 'bible'"* *[****re-****Version]* foisted by Westcott, Hort, and Strong of the aforementioned *Revised Version bible* Committee.

Strong, through his *"italics"* sleight-of-hand deception, *subtilty* removes the *Godhood of Jesus*, the *inerrancy of God's Holy Word*, *Salvation only by the blood of Jesus*, the *Trinity of God*, the *Personhood of the Holy Spirit*, a *literal Hell*, *makes Jesus synonymous with Lucifer*, and magically *changes the name of Jesus and Jehovah to the names of Lucifer's "Yeshua", "Yah", and "Yahweh"*,[241] to name but a few of his *many* assimilated deceptions!

[241] el Yerak, Dr. Rhema; Jesus and Jehovah or Yeshua and Yahweh; What Difference Does It Make What We Call God and His Son Anyway? Advanced Level Edition; chapter: The devils Who Did the Devil's Work...

Strong's Unchallenged Occultism:

James Strong's extensive article on the *occult* "*Cabala*", in volume two of his Encyclopedias, contains ***not*** even a whisper of censure against this vile system of Luciferian Jewish mysticism.

It instead schools the reader in all of the Cabala's particulars, even saying, "We find that in olden times *secret philosophical science and magic went hand in hand*." Instead of impugning the Cabala, it [*Strong's Encyclopedia* on the Evil *Cabala*] *impugns* as "*rigid*" *a literal interpretation of the Bible* and adds:

> "It is no wonder, then, if the Jewish cabalists of the latter part of the Middle Ages transmitted the conception of their science to their Christian adepts... in plain English, that they connected with it the idea that *a true cabalist must at the same time be a sorcerer*."[242]

Where did James Strong get his definitions? He took up many definitions from the ***Koran** and the books of the **Cabala***! (both *Luciferian* texts) He believed the heretical *higher critics'* Luciferian theory that the Hebrews got their *Bible* words, not from God, but from the neighboring Pagans. He cites higher critic Eichhorn to prove that the word...

> 'Babylon, seems to connected" to Babel "to confound," "but the native etymology (see the *Koran*, ii, 66) is Bab-il, "the gate of the god. He concludes, "[T]his no doubt was the original intention of appellation".

Strong Believed in a *One World Religion Under Lucifer*: *Strong*[243] became "a member of the Old Testament company of *revisers*"[244] *[**re**-Visers; **re**-Versionists].* Strong was hand-selected by American RV

---

[242] James Strong; Cyclopedia of Biblical, Theological, and Ecclesiastical Literature; vol. 2, PP. 4, 3,6, s.v. cabala.

[243] James Strong; Cyclopedia of Biblical, Theological, and Ecclesiastical Literature; vol. i, p. 595.

[244] *New Schaff-Herzog Encyclopedia of Religious Knowledge*, New York: Funk and Wagnall's Company, vol. XI, p. 115.

*[**re**-Version]* chairman Philip Schaff, *who was also a **participant** in then **new age Parliament of World Religions**.*

Like Satan the Serpent slithering along, when the egregious errors of Westcott, Hort, and Strong were discovered, and the corrupt ***Revised "Version"*** (RV) *[**re**-Version]* was exposed, it and shed its skin and slithered away *becoming the **Revised Standard** "**Version**"* (RSV) *[**re-re**-Version]*. When that was exposed, **it became the** ***New Revised Standard Version*** (NRSV) *[**re-re-re**-Version]*. *This changing of names was nothing more than the Serpent continually shedding its skin along the way. The blaspheme remains, but the Serpent is renewed!*

Same Devil, Different Name![245]

Strong's *Encyclopedia* and *Concordance* metamorphosizes Jesus Christ into... Lucifer!

In their "*deconstructed*" [***de**-Constructed*] "new" *New Greek Text*, Strong changed the name of "*Lucifer*" to "*Morning Star*" (Isaiah 14:12) to make it appear that Lucifer is the "morning star", knowing that Jesus identified Himself, as the "Morning Star"[246]! *This is the undeniable connection of Strong, Westcott, Hort to Madam Blavatsky's Luciferian Society, to which all three devils were active members and supporters!*

In this, Luciferians teach that "Satan" is not the same "person" as "Lucifer". Satan is Evil, while Lucifer, "Adam Kadmon", or spiritual "first Adam" "sacrificed" himself allowing himself to be "cast down

[245] el Yerak, Dr. Rhema; Jesus and Jehovah or Yeshua and Yahweh; What Difference Does It Make What We Call God and His Son Anyway? Advanced Level Edition; chapter: The devils Who Did the Devil's Work...

[246] Revelation 22:16.

like lightening" from Heaven to become the "first Adam" and the like "savior-messiah" of the world.[247]

A major telltale with *non-Christians* is they *always* misquote the *Bible*, the same *Bible* which they claim has no authority, they still use it in an effort to *advance their Luciferian lies*. JESUS clearly identified *Lucifer*[248] who was cast out of Heaven when iniquity was found in him. JESUS said:

> And he said unto them, I beheld *Satan* as lightning fall from heaven. (Luke 10:18)

Strong's Encyclopedia charges that *Lucifer is not Satan*, *but Lucifer is "Jesus" Christ*. Strong quotes one "Dr. Henderson," whom Strong notes, "justly remarks in his annotation:"[249] "The application of this passage [Isaiah. 14:12] to Satan, and to the fall of the apostate angels, is one of those gross [***per***-*Versions*] of Sacred Writ..."[250]

Notice the root word connection between: "***per***-*Versions*" to "*Versions*" to **re**-*Version, et al. Strong's Encyclopedia* also states that in Isaiah 14:12, the word "Lucifer" means "morning star" (*which is impossible since the Hebrew word for '**star**'[251] is **nowhere** found in Isaiah 14:12* or any of the surrounding texts).

Strong continues by saying, "The scope and connection show that none but the king of Babylon is meant, *thereby eliminating any*

[247] For a more in-depth discussion on "Adam Kadmon" as the "messiah" of occult religions: see el Yerak, Dr. Rhema; JESUS and JEHOVAH or Yeshua and Yahweh; What Difference Does It Make What We Call GOD and His Son Anyway? Advanced Level Edition; chapter: The devils Who Did the Devil's Work...; chapter: The Pagan Origin of the "god" Yahweh. Same Devil. Different Name!

[248] Ye are of your father the devil, and the lusts of your father ye will do. He was a murderer from the beginning, and abode not in the truth, because there is no truth in him. When he speaketh a lie, he speaketh of his own: for he is a liar, and the father of it. (John 8:44).

[249] GA Riplinger; *Hazardous Materials*; P. 189.

[250] James Strong; Cyclopedia of Biblical, Theological, and Ecclesiastical Literature; vol. i, p. 595.

[251] *kowkab*: Strong's H3556.

connection [*of Lucifer*] *to Satan*.

After denying that Lucifer is Satan, and that Isaiah 14 describes Lucifer's fall, *Strong's Encyclopedia blasphemously insists that Lucifer is Jesus Christ!* It quotes the apostate Delitzch saying,[252]

> In another and far higher sense, however, the designation [Lucifer, whom he believes is the morning star] was applicable to him in whom promise and fulfillment entirely corresponded, and it is so applied by Jesus when he styles himself 'The bright and *morning Star*' (Rev. xxii, 16). In a sense reign with him. See STAR.[253]

At every mention of Jesus, the Luciferians tell us that Lucifer is Jesus. The *Bible Book* of Revelation in verse 22:16, misquoted above, Jesus actually tells us plainly that Jesus ***IS*** the "***Morning Star***":

> ***I Jesus*** have sent mine angel to testify unto you these things in the churches. ***I am*** the root and the offspring of David, and ***the bright and morning star***. (Revelation 22:16)

Jesus has a special place saved in Hell for Satan and those whom attempted to *change Jesus Christ into Lucifer*:

> *Woe unto them that call evil good, **and good evil**; that put darkness for light, and light for darkness*; that put bitter for sweet, and sweet for bitter! (Isaiah 5:20)

In Conclusion, I Repeat the Introduction…

It is critical for Christians to have at least a basic understanding of how the Devil has "*crept in unawares*" infiltrating most churches, and infecting the minds of a myriad of Believers. Three of the most evil of the Devil's influencers are Westcott, Hort, and Strong… the Devil's "trinity" of Evil… *The devils Who Did the Devil's Work…*

---

[252] GA Riplinger; *Hazardous Materials*; P. 190.

[253] James Strong; Cyclopedia of Biblical, Theological, and Ecclesiastical Literature; vol. i, p. 595.

These are the three devils that did the most catastrophic work of Lies of the Devil against GOD's Word, and whose devils still haunt the Church today... There are, and have been, a most dominant confederacy of modern "'bible' critics" and "*translators*" *[**re**-Translators]* who have *quietly* woven Evil throughout the true *Bible* and created counterfeit Luciferian "'bible' *Versions*" *[**re**-Versions]*.

One should begin to smell the suffocating fumes of Sulphur rising when someone announces their intention to "criticize" the *Bible*, the Holy Words of GOD!

Book Notes

18. Appendix 3: Tongues Is **Not** *Required to Confirm Salvation:*

Tongues: *Simple*, but Not Always *Easy*...
Let's See: *What Does God Say*...

> And it came to pass, that, while Apollos was at Corinth, Paul having passed through the upper coasts came to Ephesus: and finding certain disciples, He said unto them, Have ye received the Holy Ghost [Holy Spirit] since ye believed? And they said unto him, We have not so much as heard whether there be any Holy Ghost. And he said unto them, Unto what then were ye baptized? And they said, Unto John's baptism.
>
> Then said Paul, John verily baptized with the baptism of repentance, saying unto the people, that they should believe on him which should come after him, that is, on Christ Jesus. When they heard this, they were [water] baptized in the name of the Lord Jesus. And *when Paul had laid his hands upon them,* ***the Holy Ghost came on them****; and they* ***spake with tongues, and*** *prophesied*. (Acts 19:1-6)

These 12 men were *already* "Saved", but they were not *water* baptized[254]. After each's water baptism, these Believers then received their Gift of *Tongues*. *Tongues is a rare Gift of the Holy Spirit.*

[254] For a much more in depth Study see the author's Up-coming Book: *The Three Baptisms of the New Testament: What Does God Say?*. There is much, much, more defining which will define The Three Baptisms of the New Testament. In order. If Baptism is not clearly understood, using Dr. el Yerak's: *God's Jigsaw Puzzle Bible Study Method*™ and work it out.

Tongues only confirms that Salvation has *already* occurred. Hence their new ability for their God-given ability to *Speak In Tongues*.

These did not "*Speak In Tongues*" until ***sometime after*** **Salvation** had already occurred. In fact, there are many Christians who fail to ever release their *Tongues* before they die, and will still be found in Heaven. Probably the most stark example of this is the thief crucified next to Jesus on the Cross. Jesus said emphatically:

> And Jesus said unto him, Verily I say unto thee, To day shalt thou be with me in paradise. (Luke 23:43)

This error comes from putting the cart before the horse. Or as the adage goes, What comes first, the chicken or the egg? (Just for Fun... The chicken came first!) False doctrines emanate from people pretending to be "god" having a self-anointed "doctrine". Acting in their self-delusion, trying to reverse engineer their errant beliefs. Remember, "*praying in tongues*" does <u>*not*</u> exist.

A person must be Born-Again, Saved, before they can "*Speak In Tongues*" or "*Pray in the Spirit*". But, "*Speaking in Tongues*", as we have seen, is a "*Gift*" of the Holy Spirit that *only given a very limited number of Believers*. Tongues are given for others and <u>*not*</u> Ourselves.

"*Praying In the Spirit*" is for <u>***all***</u> Believers individually. We can see that the *confusion* caused by lumping these 2 Doctrines together, *confusion* always ensues. It ensues to the point of wrecking many a Believer's Faith. This echoes a previous point that trying to discern Scriptures above your maturity level... can shipwreck a Believer's Faith.

Tongues Not Required™©[255]

Prayer Language Also is *NOT* Required for Salvation: There are many First Century Believers that are not recorded in There are many First

[255] *Subject Tracking Boxes* are ™ and © by Third Awakening Foundation Inc.

Century Believers that are not recorded in Scripture as ever having had their *Tongues* released. If it were required for Salvation, then God would certainly have mentioned and emphasized it... repeatedly. *Correct*?

Not all Christians ever experience Speaking In Tongues, but they are still Saved and either Heaven bound, or already in Heaven. If "Speaking In Tongues" were required to "prove" Salvation, then all of the Old Testament Saints would still be trapped in Hell! There was not yet possession of the Holy Spirit in the Believer's spirit, the very definition of Salvation in the Old testament:

> *For by grace are ye saved through faith; and that not of yourselves: it is the gift of God: Not of works, lest any man should boast. (Ephesians 2:8-9)*

Becoming a Christian is by the Grace alone. There are no Christians who worked to receive, nor maintain Salvation. Don't let the God-Mockers fool you with confusion and complexity!

This falls in the do not cherry-pick God's Word category. You cannot take a cherry-picked phrase and make a Doctrine from it. There is no such emphasis in Scripture. It is true that many First Century Believers did have a *Prayer Language*, but certainly *not* all.

Everything Must Align with Scripture

Salvation is by *Grace* alone. If Baptism were required, then it would be a *work of men*, and not of God, to be boasted about for the *Believer's work to achieve Salvation. A form of making oneself a "co-god"* Let's take a deeper look at Ephesians 2:8-9:

> For *by grace are ye saved through faith* [Grace and nothing more]; and that *not of yourselves*: it is the ***gift*** *of God*: *Not of **works**, lest any man should **boast***. (Ephesians 2:8-9)

This is a sort of "**works Salvation**", by which a Believer must manifest "*Tongues*" to "prove" Salvation. Unfortunately, this necessarily leads to a multitude of "*pretenders*". Pretenders not wanting to be kicked out of fellowship. *Salvation is wholly about what Jesus did*, it is a **Gift**, and *not what we can do to earn, or keep it*. If the Believer is at least, even in part, responsible for their own Salvation, Believers would have "**boasting rights**" *making themselves* equal with "God"! (*Not today Satan, Not today!*)

As previously stated, "*praying in tongues*" ***is not Biblical***, making the whole discussion of "*praying In tongues*"... *moot*. (Remember there is *no such thing as "praying in tongues"* as wrongfully misinterpreted by many misguided churches who are intentionally, or naïvely, following Luciferian Helena Blavatsky.)

However, "*Praying In the Spirit*" is a sign of being Baptized by the Holy Spirit. ***The Holy Spirit "In" a Believer is what makes the Believer Born-Again***[256], *"Saved"*; ***The Holy Spirit "On" a Believer is anointing and Empowerment for Ministry***. To be Baptized by the Holy Spirit can *only* happen to a Born-Again Believer.[257]

---

[256] (John 3:1-8).

[257] See upcoming Book: el Yerak, Dr. Rhema; *Trinity of God: What Does God Say?* Publication date TBA.

Speaking in Tongues, or an earthly foreign Language not spoken by a Believer, is a *Gift of the Holy Spirit*. You do not pay for "gifts". *Gifts are free, or they are not gifts at all…*
In conclusion, *Not all Christians experience Speaking In Tongues, but they are still Saved and Heaven bound. If "Speaking In Tongues" were required to "prove" Salvation, then all of the Old Testament Saints would be forever trapped in Hell! There was not yet possession of the Holy Spirit in the Believer's spirit, the very definition of Salvation.*

*As the Bible makes clear using **God's Bible Puzzle Study Method**™, Speaking In Tongues is NOT required for Salvation.*

Book Notes

19. Appendix 4: To Know That You Know...

To Know That You Know...

There is no greater question to be answered than:
... Sirs, what must I do to be saved? (Acts 16:30)

How you choose to answer this question will determine where you will spend eternity... in Heaven with God, or in Hell in the eternal punishment of *Hell-fire*.

How To Meet Jesus. What Must I Do To Be Saved?

- The Way to Salvation is in Jesus alone. (Acts 4:12)
- To be Saved is to be Born-Again in your spirit by God the Holy Spirit (John 3:1-8)
- You must submit yourself wholly to Jesus as your God *and* your Savior. (2 Peter 1:1)
- All it takes is a honest 30-second prayer to God... Are you ready?

Are you Saved?

Here is a good measure on whether you are *actually* Saved and going to Heaven...

How is it that you can *know that you know* if you have ever ***act**ually* been Saved, and are in fact going to Heaven, what Jesus calls "Born-Again"? Well let's use a little story that God gave me to investigate this question with you...

The Knock at the Door...

Imagine that it's Saturday morning and you are watching some brainless cartoons on TV to decompress from the hectic week. Suddenly there is a knock at the front door. Knock, knock, knock... Oh crap, you mumble quietly under your breath. Very stealthily you creep to the window and slightly draw back the edge of the window curtain.

You don't want to get caught because everyone knows who the early Saturday morning unsolicited visit generally comes from! But to your shock it is not that kind of visitor! You go to the peep-hole in the front door to get a second look.

No this can't be you tell yourself! You then open the door just so slightly, and sure enough it's the President of the United States standing at *your* front door! "Mr. President!", you barely manage to sputter out as you swing your door open.

The President says hello and apologizes for showing up unannounced. The President calls you by name and says that his Presidency has run into a bit of a problem because some of the people do not think that he fully appreciates the struggles of the common man.

His advisors, he says, tell him that he should move in with an average family and get acquainted with the hardships of the common man... and I have chosen you!, the President says. In your mind you are thinking "Wow! the President living at my house!". But out-loud you say, it would be an honor Mr. President.

The next Monday the President and his wife move into your back bedroom with his advisors, staff, and other dignitaries filing in and out at all hours. On Tuesday you tell the President that on Friday nights you have your buddies over and play poker, a tradition that you have continued since high school. You inquire if you could still keep your tradition given this change of circumstances.

The President replies that of course, and if you were willing, I would love to also sit in and play. You tell the President that that would be great! Your friends are excited to not only meet the President, but to play poker with him every Friday night!

Over the next several years the President faithfully attends the poker games when he is not out of town on official business. It is great to have the President inquire of you on every major domestic policy decision that he has on his agenda. He really listens and takes every word to heart.

At the end of his second-term the President has been "term-limited out" and cannot run again. He shakes your hand and gives you a buddy-hug and thanks you for your service to him, and to your Country. "Wow!", you say… which takes you back to the same expression where it all started.

Now here is the question: Could it *ever* be possible, as you and your buddies continue playing poker every Friday night, that one of your buddies would begin to reminisce about how you all played poker with the President of the United States; Would it be possible that you could not remember when the President knocked on your front door and you invited him in to live in your house?

Of course not! Not a chance!

Well here is the ultimate point: If you could *never* forget the moment that the President of the United States knocked on your door and you invited him to move into your house… then how could you *ever* forget the moment that God Himself knocked on the door of your heart and you invited the GOD of the Universe to move into your heart?

It would be absolutely *impossible* to forget that GOD had moved into your heart! JESUS said, "Behold, I stand at the *door*, and knock: if any man hear my voice, and open the door, *I will come in to him*, and will sup with him, and he with me". (Revelation 3:20)

Now if you cannot remember the exact moment that you asked GOD to move into your heart and you accepted JESUS as your GOD and Savior, then you are *not* a Born-Again Christian! (I am not talking about you remembering the exact time of the day, or month, or year, but the that exact *moment* somewhere in your past.) Without this *moment* of surrender, you are *not* headed to Heaven, but tragically you are headed for eternal damnation in the flames of Hell.

The *Bible* is clear that there is only *one* way to become a Christian.

> Jesus saith unto him, *I am the way, the truth, and the life: no man cometh unto the Father, but by me*. (John 14:6)

How Do I Know, that I Know, that I'm Saved?

The Man on the Shore:

I liken the deciding moment which leads to Salvation to a man being swept down a raging river in his canoe towards certain doom of a treacherous waterfall. The man can hear the coming waterfall and certain death awaiting him several hundred feet below his viewable horizon, being thrown onto the sharp jagged rocks below.

The man's boat is loaded down with every one of the man's accumulated sins, all of which he is holding onto tightly with a death-grip.

There is a second Man standing on the shore with a rope capable of saving him from eminent death. The man in the canoe screams out to the Man on the shore, "please save me from certain death!". The Man on the shore throws the rope which lands across the bow of the little canoe. The Man on the shore calls out, "I will be your God and your Savior!".

The man in the boat looks quite puzzled; this is not the deal which he expected and calls back, "I just want a savior". The Man on the shore calls back, "your grip will not hold unless you abandon all of your sins and throw yourself overboard and wholly trust in Me to Save you.

Now let go of your sins, grab hold of the rope, and jump out of your boat... and I will pull you to safety".

The man in the canoe calls back, "No, I just want to be Saved, but I want no commitment beyond that". The Man on the shore desperately calls back to the man in the canoe headed ever closer to certain death, "My Father has set me here to Save you, but because of the terrible price which it cost Me to be positioned here, My Father demands that you leave all sin behind, or you cannot be Saved".

Hearing this the man in the canoe turns his head away and mutters to himself, "I just wanted to be rescued, but I will not leave all of my life's acquired sins behind". The man in the canoe drops his head and blocks out the pleading cries of the Savior from the shore.

The man in the canoe refused to give up his boatload of accumulated sins, and determined that he would hold onto them until the very end, which was fast approaching. The man was neither saved, nor rescued. This is a tragic allegory, but one that is repeated millions of times every day! People want to be saved, but not submitted to God. Again, with God you are either *all-in*... or *all-out*!

This is the same decision that we must *all* face. We have a choice between our sins... and Salvation. Too many people want to be saved from the eminent doom of Hell, but still want to cling to the Evil of their sins. Sin cannot enter Heaven... into the very presence of GOD the Father. It's simply... *impossible.*

Hell is full of those who loved their sin, rather than GOD. Salvation is a package deal. You must accept JESUS Christ as your GOD *and* your Savior. To be Born-Again you *must* first accept JESUS as GOD, you "must Believe that he [JESUS] is [GOD]".

> But without faith it is impossible to please him [GOD]: for he that cometh to God **must believe that he** [JESUS] **is** [**God**], and that he is a rewarder of them that diligently seek him. (Hebrews 11:6).

In return you receive a package deal from GOD receiving God the Father, God the Son, and God the Holy Spirit. One GOD in Three Persons. It's a great deal, but there is a cost... you must wholly surrender your life and sins to JESUS as your God!

The Commitment to JESUS takes less than 30 seconds...

If you have not yet accepted JESUS as your God and Savior, please consider doing so now. This is the Salvation which JESUS paid the ultimate price for on the Cross to buy you back from the Devil, Hell, and your sin.

The prayer takes less than 30 seconds. Now is the moment to accept Jesus as your God and Savior and put your heart on the Way to Heaven! Again, this commitment takes *less than 30 seconds*.

All that is required is that you Believe that Jesus *is* God, you are a sinner in need of a Savior, Jesus died for your sins, and that Jesus raised Himself from the dead three days later. Then simply pray and tell Jesus:

The Prayer of Salvation:

Jesus, I wholly surrender my life to You as my God and Savior. Jesus, I am a sinner. I need a Savior. I surrender all of my sins to you Jesus and ask You for Your Forgiveness of all my sins. I accept Your Salvation and thank You for Dying on the Cross to Save me. In Jesus name, Amen!

That's it. If you've done that and mean that with all your heart ... Congratulations! You are now a Christian, and as such, a Born-Again child of God! If you have made the decision to accept Jesus as your God and Savior and have become a Born-Again Christian, we would love to hear from you about your experience!

Salvation@ThirdAwakeningFoundation.com

Welcome to the Kingdom of God!

Book Notes

20. Appendix 5- Lineage of the Received Text Bible (KJB)

Lineage of the *Received Text, King James Bible from Day of Pentecost to Today:*

Compiled by Dr. Ken Matto:
The *King James Bible* has a very GODly lineage dating back to the original autographs and has been transmitted to us through the ages without corruption because GOD promised that His Word would be preserved by Himself so subsequent generations of Christians would have the same authoritative words as the Early Church.

Below are the names of the earlier [translations] of which the *King James Bible* drew its incorruption from. If you have a pastor in your church that discards the *King James Bible* as inferior to other *Bible* Translations, then he has been seriously deceived. If the KJB was inferior would GOD have used it to literally evangelize the world?

THE OLD TESTAMENT

1524-25 Bomberg Edition of the Masoretic Text also known as the Ben Chayyim Text

THE NEW TESTAMENT

All dates are Anno Domini (A.D.)

30-95------------Original Autographs
95-150----------Greek Vulgate (Copy of Originals)
120---------------The Waldensian *Bible*
150---------------The Peshitta (Syrian Copy)
150-400-------- Papyrus Readings of the Receptus
157-------------- The Italic *Bible* - From the Old Latin Vulgate used in Northern Italy
157-------------- The Old Latin Vulgate
177-------------- The Gallic *Bible*
310-------------- The Gothic Version of Ulfilas

350-400------- The Textus Receptus is Dominant Text
400-------------- Augustine favors Textus Receptus
400-------------- The Armenian *Bible* (Translated by Mesrob)
400-------------- The Old Syriac
450-------------- The Palestinian Syriac Version
450-1450------ Byzantine Text Dominant (Textus Receptus)
508-------------- Philoxenian - by Chorepiscopos Polycarp, who commissioned by Philoxenos of Mabbug
500-1500------ Uncial Readings of Receptus (Codices)
616-------------- Harclean Syriac (Translated by Thomas of Harqel – Revision of 508 Philoxenian)
864-------------- Slavonic
1100-1300---- The Latin *Bible* of the Waldensians (History goes back as far as the 2nd century as people of the Vaudoix Valley)
1160------------ The Romaunt Version (Waldensian)
1300-1500---- The Latin *Bible* of the Albigenses
1382-1550---- The Latin *Bible* of the Lollards
1384------------ The Wycliffe *Bible*
1516------------ Erasmus's First Edition Greek New Testament
1522------------ Erasmus's Third Edition Published
1522-1534---- Martin Luther's German *Bible*
1525------------ Tyndale Version
1534------------ Tyndale's Amended Version
1534------------ Colinaeus' Receptus
1535------------ Coverdale Version
1535------------ Lefevre's French *Bible*
1537------------ Olivetan's French *Bible*
1537------------ *Matthew's Bible* (John Rogers Printer)
1539------------ *Taverner's Bible*
1539------------ The *Great Bible*
1541------------ Swedish Upsala *Bible* by Laurentius
1550------------ Stephanus Receptus (St. Stephen's Text)
1550------------ Danish Christian III *Bible*
1558------------ Biestken's Dutch Work

1560------------ The *Geneva Bible*
1565------------ Theodore Beza's Receptus
1568------------ The *Bishop's Bible*
1569------------ Spanish Translation by Cassiodoro de Reyna
1587------------ *Geneva Bible* ("Imprinted at London by Christopher Barker, Printer to the Qveenes Maiestie. 1587 Cum priuilegio.")
1598------------ Theodore Beza's Text
1602------------ Czech Version
1607------------ Diodati Italian Version
1611------------ The *King James Bible* with Apocrypha between Old and New Testament
1613------------ The *King James Bible* (Apocrypha Removed) **(2)**
1769------------ 4th update of the English Language in the King James *Bible*

We have in our possession today the 4th update of the 1769 *King James, Received Text Bible*. It was done to update the English language only. No translation work was done.

Book Notes

21. Appendix 6: The Third Awakening Foundation:

Third Awakening Foundation

The Third Awakening Foundation was established primarily to lead lost souls to Salvation, which only comes through accepting JESUS as God and Savior[258]. And secondly, helping Believers reach the fullest possible point of Maturity in JESUS Christ through God the Holy Spirit. The primary way of the perfection of GOD's children is *Discipleship*.

We present the "Fundamentals" of JESUS' Born-Again Salvation in the chapter, *To Know That You Know...* Then from the Fundamentals we are, "leaving the principles of the doctrine of Christ" and we will, "go on unto perfection". Too many Churches get stuck in the Fundamentals and never *go on unto the perfection of the Believer...* without Discipleship it leaves the Believer marooned without the navigation skills necessary to live a GODly Christian life.

Not being Discipled is a key reason that Christians are never able to *Grow Up!*[259] This is what the *Bible* refers to when Paul laments the Christians who are always needing the "milk" of babies in the Fundamentals of Salvation, and are *never* Discipled with the meat of the Gospel. Paul was frustrated at the Church at Corinth who never wanted to mature in Christ JESUS and constantly demanded the milk of easy Christianity.[260]

[258] See final chapter in this Book: *To Know That You Know...*

[259] The title of an upcoming Book *Grow Up! What Does God Say?* by this author Rev. Dr. Rhema el Yerak, Sr. Print date TBA.

[260] 1 Corinthians 3:2-3.

A Believer's inability to function as a mature Christian most often stems from a stagnant Church environment. The postmodern Church has been disemboweled of its *Authority* in Jesus' name by the hidden movements of witchcraft, occultism, and Luciferianism.

God says, Christians are destroyed from a lack of knowledge[261] of God's maturing process. The Christian's maturity comes in large part through Discipleship. At the Third Awakening Foundation it is our heart and intent to see the Body of Christ Discipled into a working maturity available for every Believer.

The Third Awakening Foundation is focused on bringing the lost to Salvation in Christ Jesus, and then helping Born-Again Believers mature into the person that Christ Jesus intended them to become. We strive to make available the *Bible*-based Discipleship for those Christians who desire to let God perfect them more-and-more so that all the world may see the image of Jesus Christ fully reflected through us. A blessed and joyous life is only possible in this process of becoming more like Jesus.

Dr. Rhéma el Yérak, DDiv

[261] My people are destroyed for lack of knowledge: because thou hast rejected knowledge, I will also reject thee, that thou shalt be no priest to me: seeing thou hast forgotten the law of thy God, I will also forget thy children. (Hosea 4:6).

Other Third Awakening Foundation Titles:
by Dr. Rhéma el Yérak:

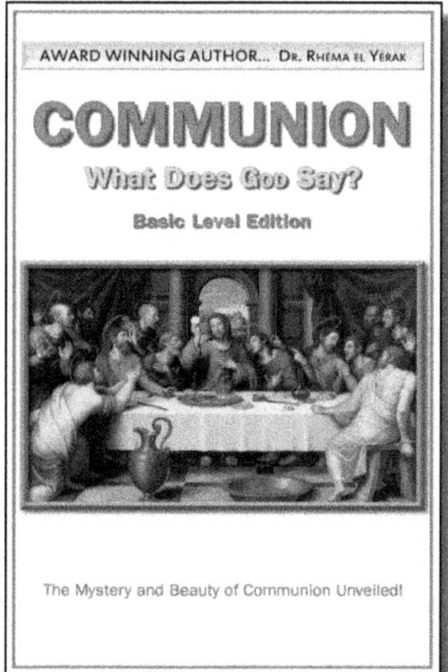

Also available on Amazon! and www.ThirdAwakeningFoundation.com

Book Notes

22. Appendix 7: MeetJesus.Info

Third Awakening Foundation, Inc.

www.ingramcontent.com/pod-product-compliance
Lightning Source LLC
LaVergne TN
LVHW010615100826
845148LV00014B/2983